five stages of ~~grief~~ *love*

aridam s. dojie

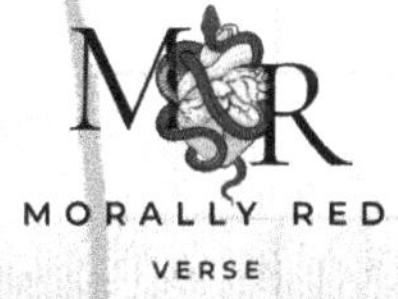

Morally Red Verse
An imprint of Aridam S. Dojie
www.asdojie.com

Five Stages of Love
First Edition, October 2024

ISBN 978-81-977830-2-9 (Paperback)
ISBN 978-81-977830-4-3 (Hardcover)
ISBN 978-81-977830-9-8 (e-Book)

To the quiet, little girl in my mirror.
It's okay to use your voice now.
I've got you.

And to you, dear reader,
and the little person in your mirror too.
It's okay. You've got you.

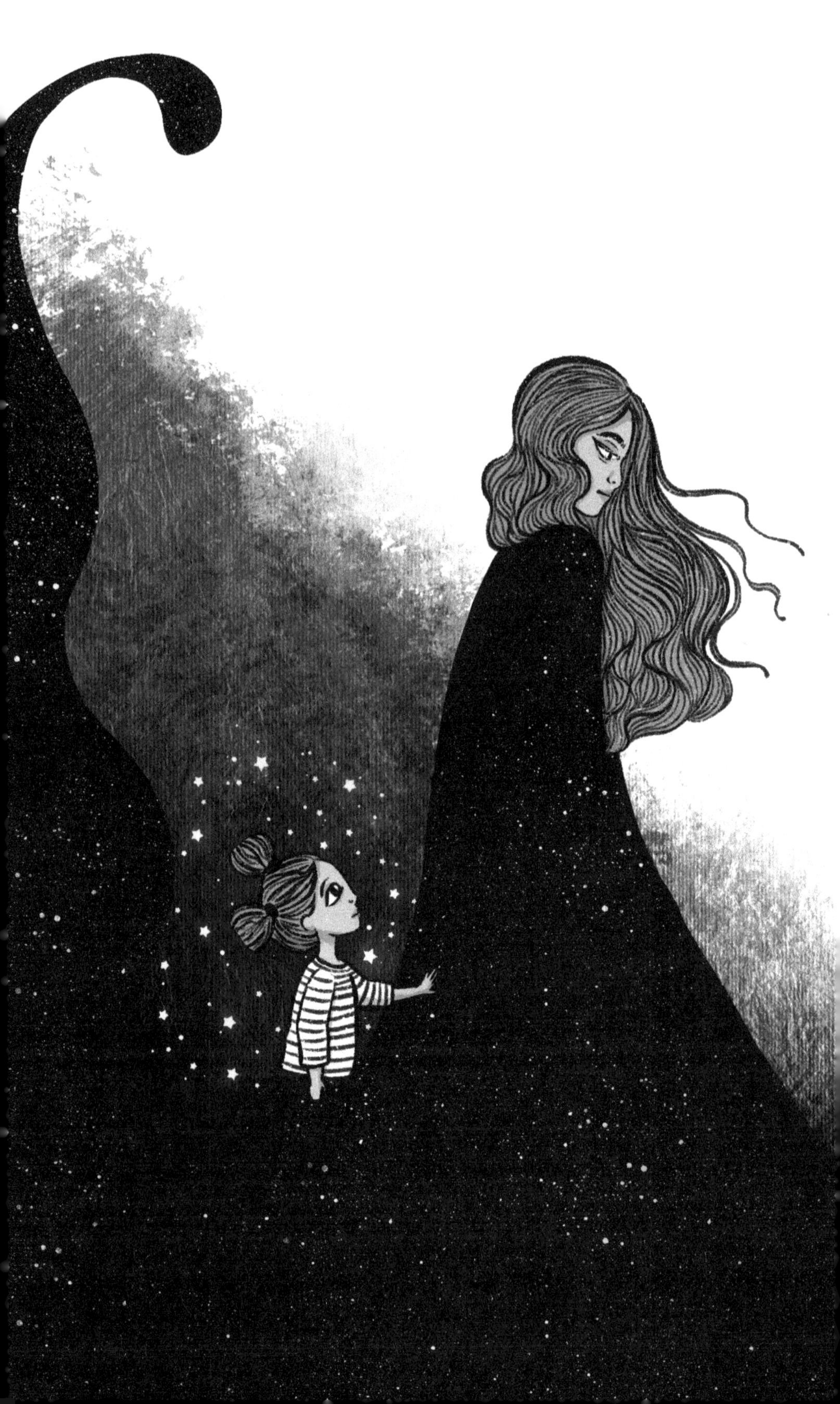

*d*ear reader,

I had been sitting with grief for a while, intellectualizing it, because apparently, it's a thing we humans do, so we don't have to feel our feelings — we intellectualize them. And that's exactly what I did, even as I worked on feeling all those feelings to process the pesky little thing through its five dreaded stages of denial, anger, bargain, depression, and finally, acceptance. All while also slowly marinating in its own juices, it morphed into something else. Something I didn't quite understand at the time, but something that stuck and stayed, and eventually brought me face to face with this other, far more formidable emotion that required processing in its own right: *love*

Surely, it must have its own logical stages too. Because how else do you even begin to process love through this intense enemies-to-lovers dance in a generations-old war, where it's always you against you — your nemesis number one? And also, because what is love but the other side of grief? Especially the love that blooms after it. The love that is warmth, forever withheld from the inner-most reaches of our hearts. The love that is found to be an oddity, if ever witnessed by our broken-most parts.

The love that originally belonged to the detested child in a now adult body, abandoned for far too long for her to be even acquainted with the emotion anymore. And the love that still belongs to her, for she has been clinging to it without knowing why her fists have remained clenched to this day.

This child, this little girl in my mirror had been holding on with a desperate desire to be loved, to be held, to be seen. It constantly seeped from every pore of her being, beckoning — its scent too obvious to predators, while the one who should've known, remained oblivious.

I refused to see her. After all, what had she done to deserve a loving gaze? What made her worthy of receiving a glance acknowledging her presence? What condition did she fulfill to be deemed *enough*?

By the time I realized how none of those conditions were mine, and that the hate was all taught, it was too late.

I wanted to see her, but she no longer wished to be seen. I craved to hear her voice, but she didn't speak anymore. I didn't know if she was mad at me or if I had really, truly lost her.

When, in the depths of our combined lows, I looked into the mirror one evening — something I've always despised — and I started talking.

"I don't know how to love you yet. But if you let me, I'll learn," I spoke to her. "Would you remind me of the dreams we used to have — dreams I've long forgotten? And will you tell me what *you* want? Whatever it is, your wish is my command." I asked her again the next day, and the day after that, and the day after that. I kept asking, only to be met with silence each time.

In all honesty though, if my mirror actually had started talking back, I would've sh*t myself right there. No kidding.

But metaphorically speaking, as all poetry does, I only realized after weeks of her silence, she'd already been answering everything. In verse, the cheeky one. And she had a lot to say. And to that, I had a lot to say.

And thus formed the raw beginnings of this book. Gathering in bits and pieces, all the mismatched fragments of our heart, ripped out over time from beneath our ribs, just so they could be sewn back together again. Whether to heal or to merely prolong our suffering, neither of us knew at the time. But now...

Now, we'd like to invite you to witness this odd collection of poetry and art, originally scribbled in random old notebooks, and on the underside of tender wrists, and on dirty napkins after spicy meals, and on coffee receipts and grocery lists, and that one time etched onto an extra pink moon with fingertips that fluttered like moths privy to our secrets, we warmly invite you — adult you and little you — together, to the Five Stages of Love.

Full disclaimer though, it gets dark, and it gets worse, before it gets better. But it does get better, I promise. Only, we need to process some stubborn sh*t first.

So, gently, lovingly — get in loser, we're processing.

love,

Ari

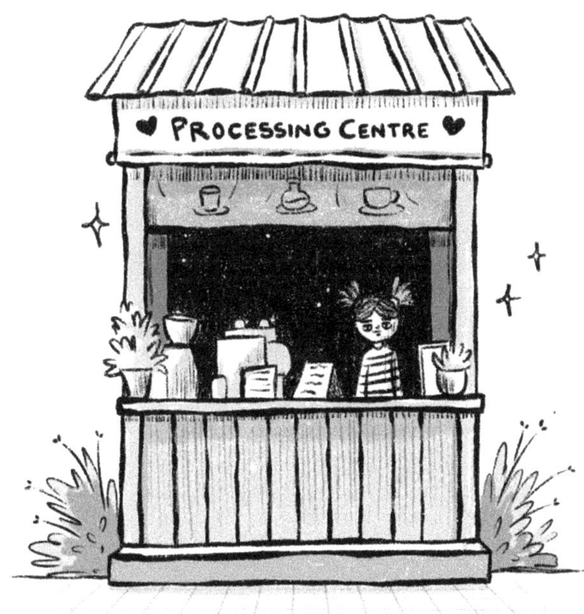

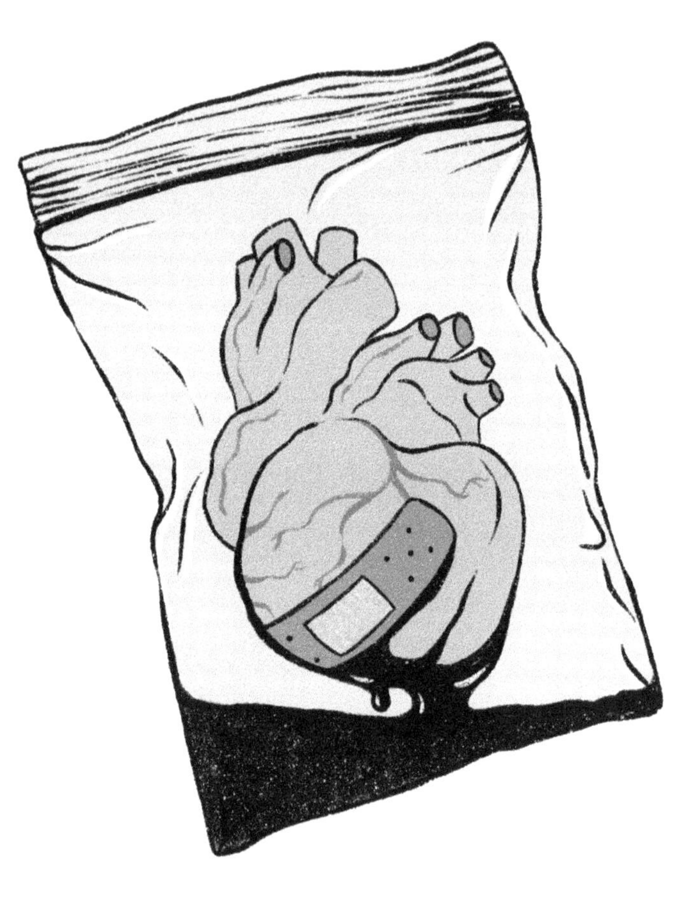

before we can truly love ourselves,
we must fully grieve ourselves

we must grieve all our versions
real and unreal
inherited or taught
learnt or lost

grieve the depths of our shadows
hidden in plain sight
along the elusive,
yet unwavering light

grieve our pasts
and all their deaths
and all their births
and all their mess

grieve, we must
so we may live
and so we may love
we must first grieve.

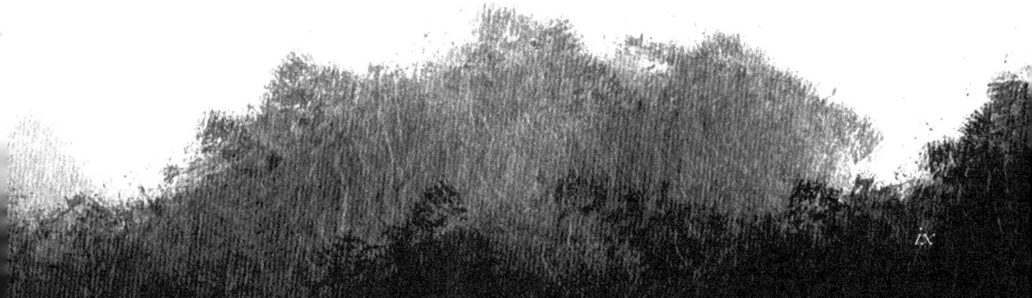

Contents

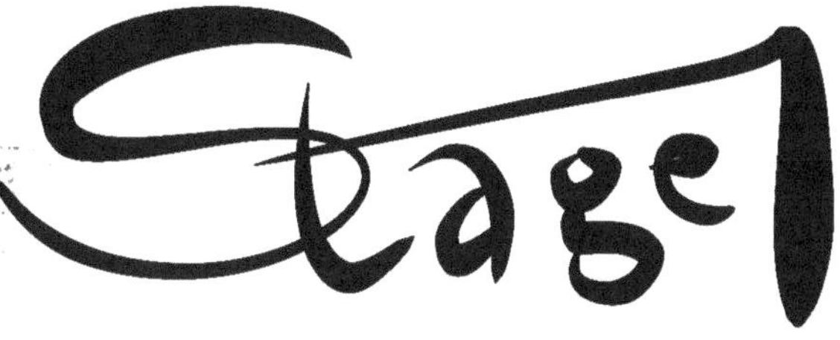

ROCK BOTTOM

— she dies —

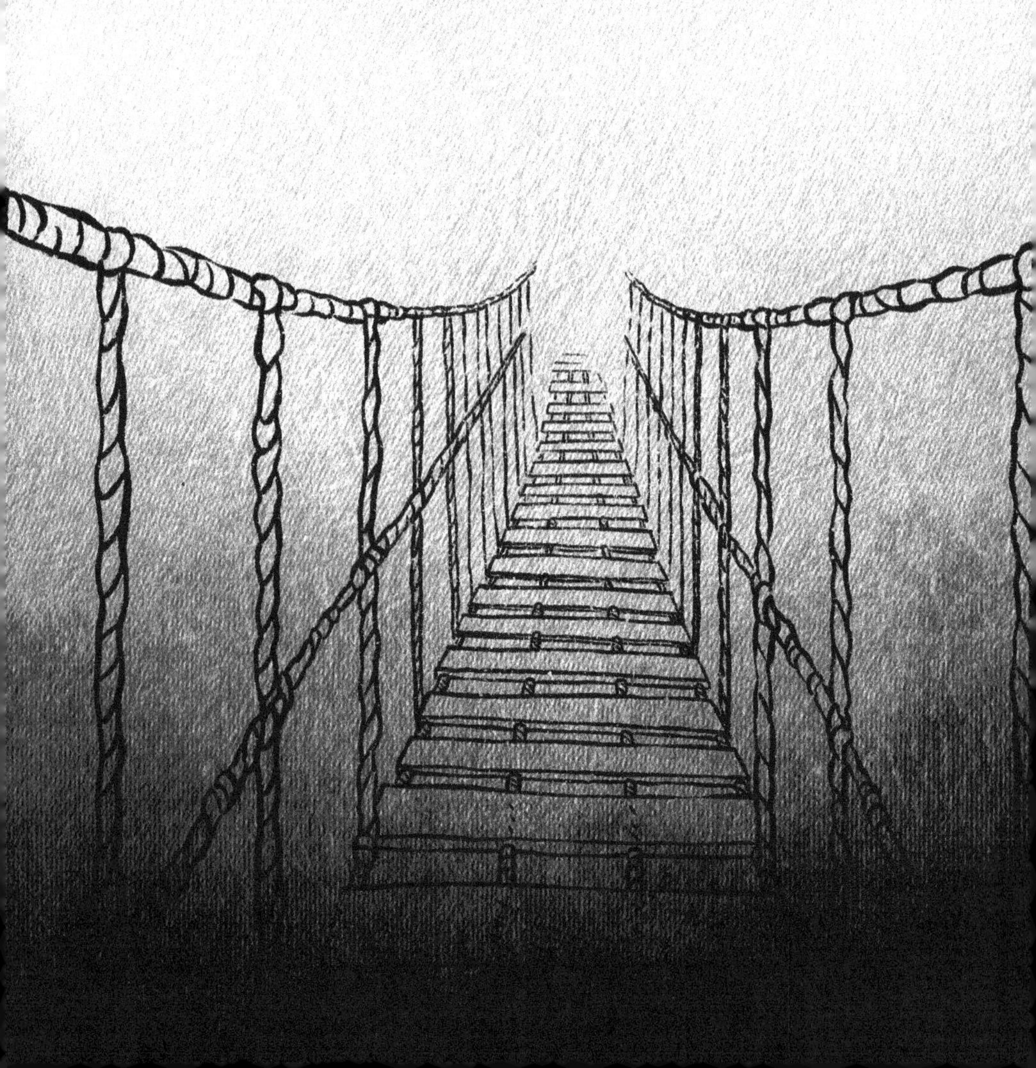

*b*ridges

you shook the bridge
so she set it on fire
watch her pour gasoline
it's her own damned pyre

names, games, crackling flames
up up up they go
sparks, heat, and soot
nothing remains anymore

except for the memories,
regrets of her trusting you
ashes of her soul
rotting corpses of the kisses she gave too

she thought she was afraid of being lonely
but she was lonelier with you
you thought she would guard it with her life
'cause she was nothing without you

but with every mark on her body
yellow, purple, blue
she watched it slowly crumble
before she burned it down for good

now she carries a match in her pocket
everywhere she goes
never really liked bridges
but you already know.

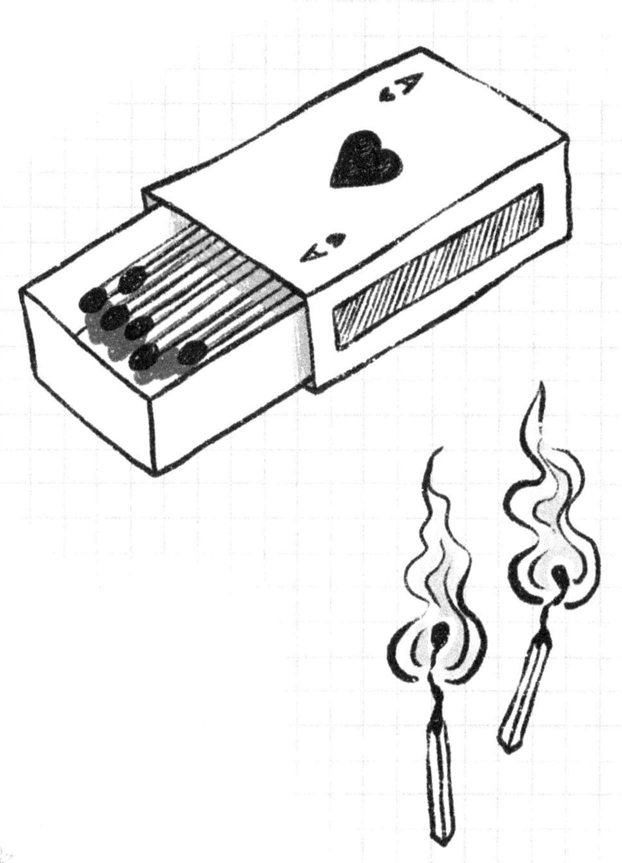

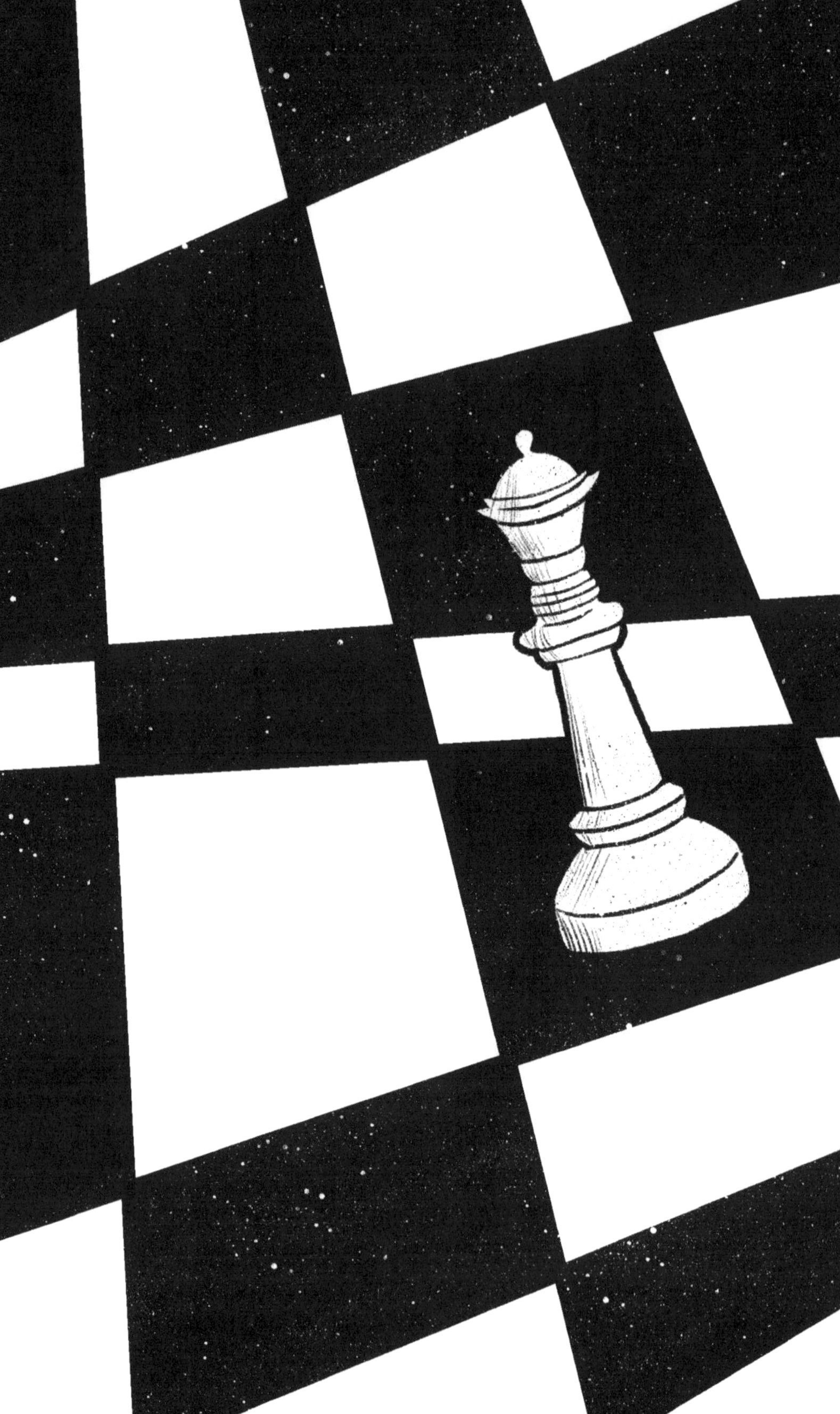

*f*estering

she sees you across the room
and just like that, she's an open wound
festering
she's festering

a stone wall
she's made of gray rocks
but inside, she's crumbling
flashbacks
from wars that weren't hers
she's frozen

she sees you across the room
and they tell her it's time
the bass in your voice
sends chills down her spine
numb hands
quicksand
she's sinking

they tell her it's over
they tell her to go
she'd move
but her limbs are too cold

she's a stone wall
the gray rocks stacked high
but inside, deep inside
she's terrified

in her brain
she's there again
trapped, broken, dead
dead, but not quite yet

she sees you across the room
and again, she's an open wound
hyper aware of the exits,
there are two
she doesn't trust her feet, the scars all itch
she wants to rip her skin off, till her blood runs blue

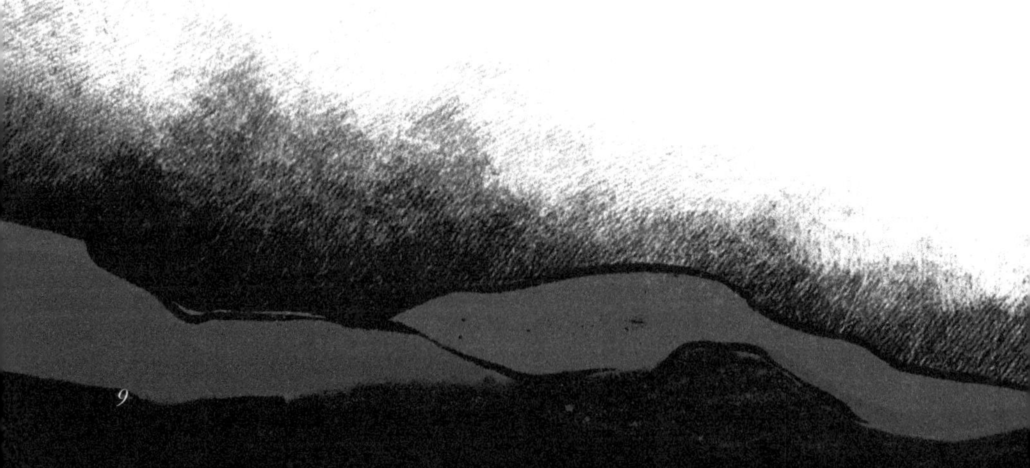

they tell her it's over
she knows, she can read
she's all too aware
how she should be relieved

but she's choking on air
and her throat's gone dry
no water, the cap won't turn
might as well swallow her cry

she already crumbled long ago
when the wretched tower fell
now she's the stone wall
and the kiln in her personal hell

these gray rocks don't crack
but harden with every crease
they tell her it's over
they tell her to go
finally, she leaves.

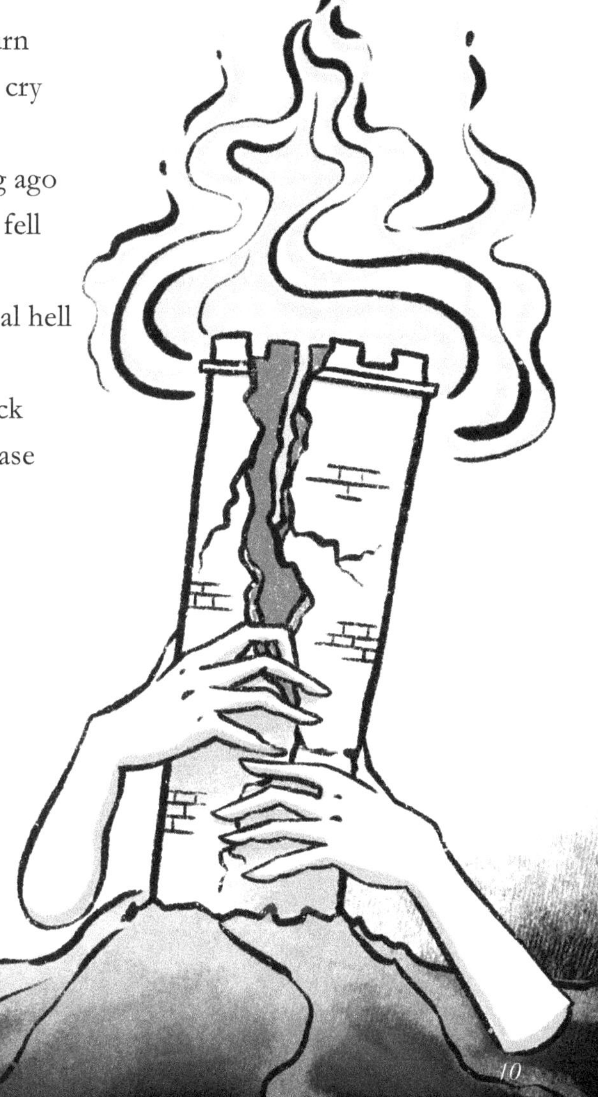

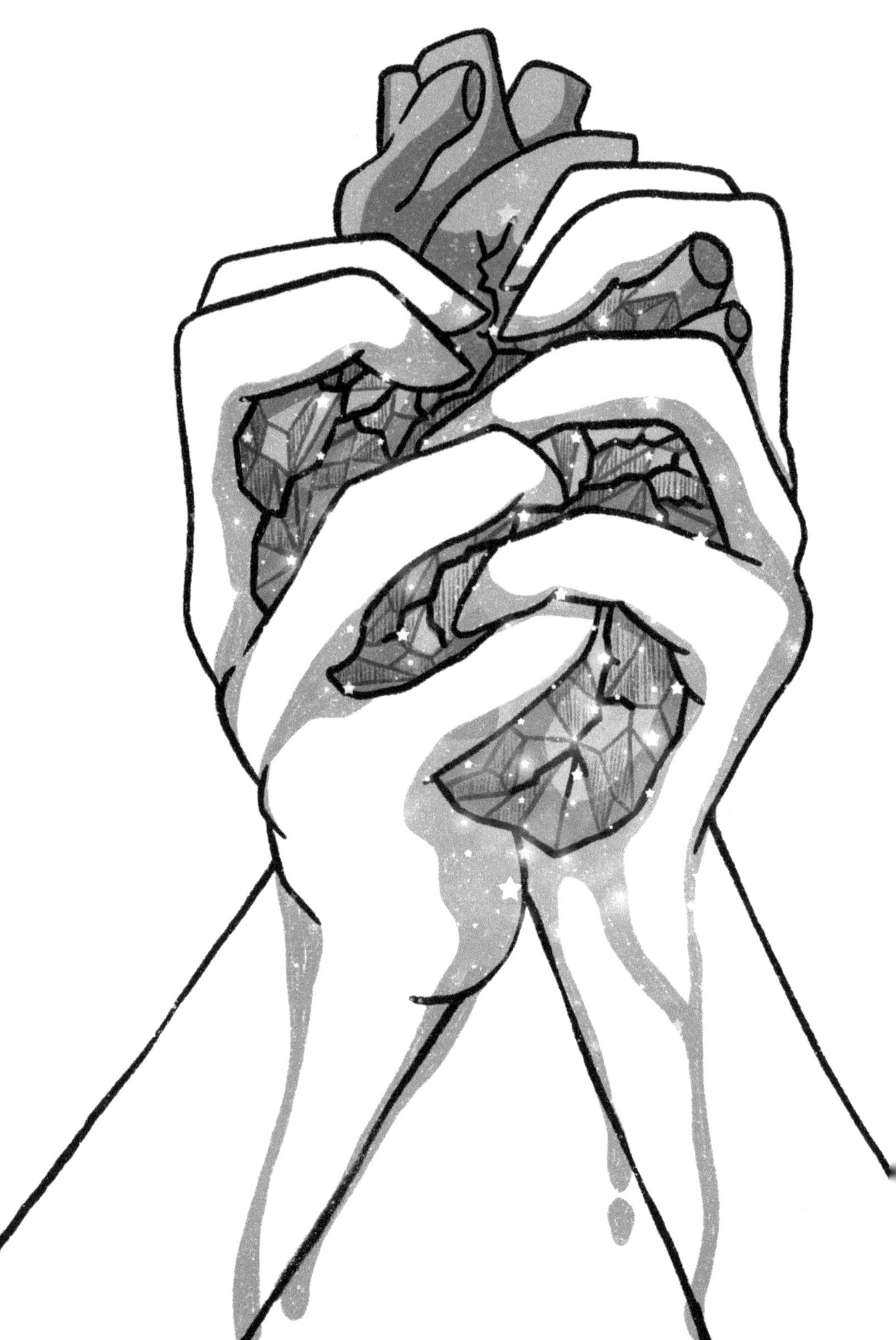

Cracks

her heart's bejeweled in blisters
bruised an ugly blue
veinous formations of gold-filled cracks
years later, they still seep an inky hue.

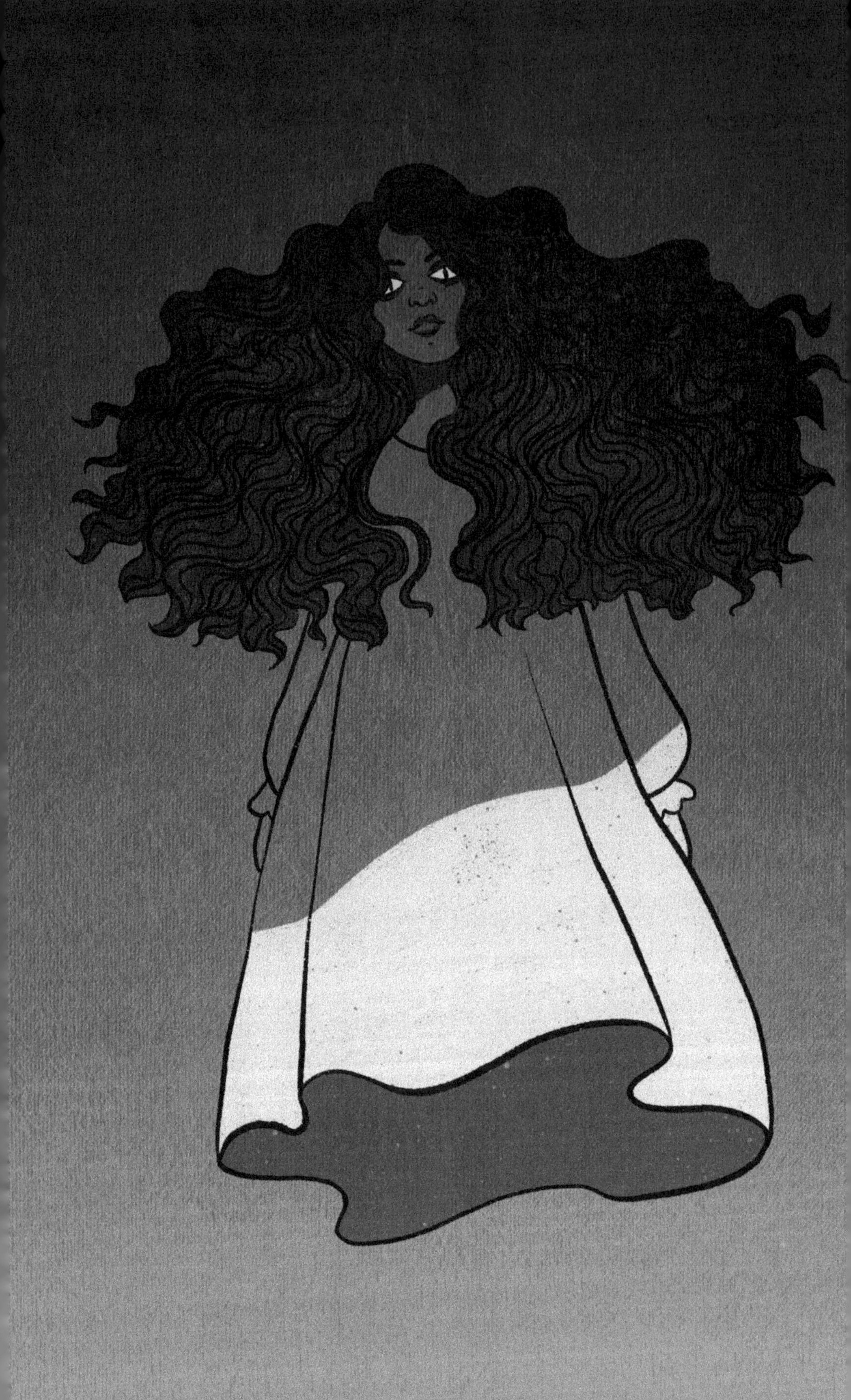

haunting

do you still sit and stare at the corner of your bed she haunts
rocking back and forth in the lull her absence left?

in company, do you still pretend she's the monster?
like you did with others before her?

you know she knows
you know she knows you know
and that's how she knows
she doesn't pity you anymore

debris, ghosts and memories
echoes of everything broken
just as every solemn promise
ever written, ever spoken

racing heartbeats and tender bones
and cracked screens of old phones
the special brand of volatile sh*t
that only rears its head behind a closed door
the charmer is all they'll ever see
with all the smokes and mirrors, and masks you wore

"thank you,"
does her ghost still whisper every time you look?
with everything you took?

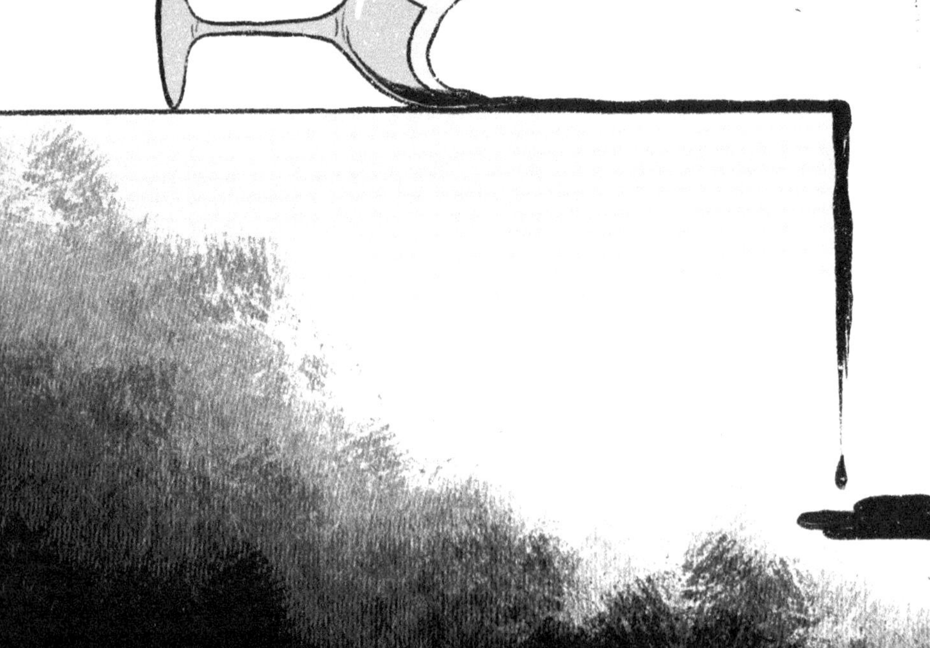

she'd do it again, you know
if she had to go back in time
because if she'd never been under your spell
to be shattered like a glass of cheap wine
she'd have never met her, the girl in her mirror
antifragile, power, divine

and when the stench of those insidious games
clear themselves a twisted debt
with all her useless possessions
and treasured trash that you kept

tell me now
don't be shy
do you still sit and stare
at the corners of your withering mind?

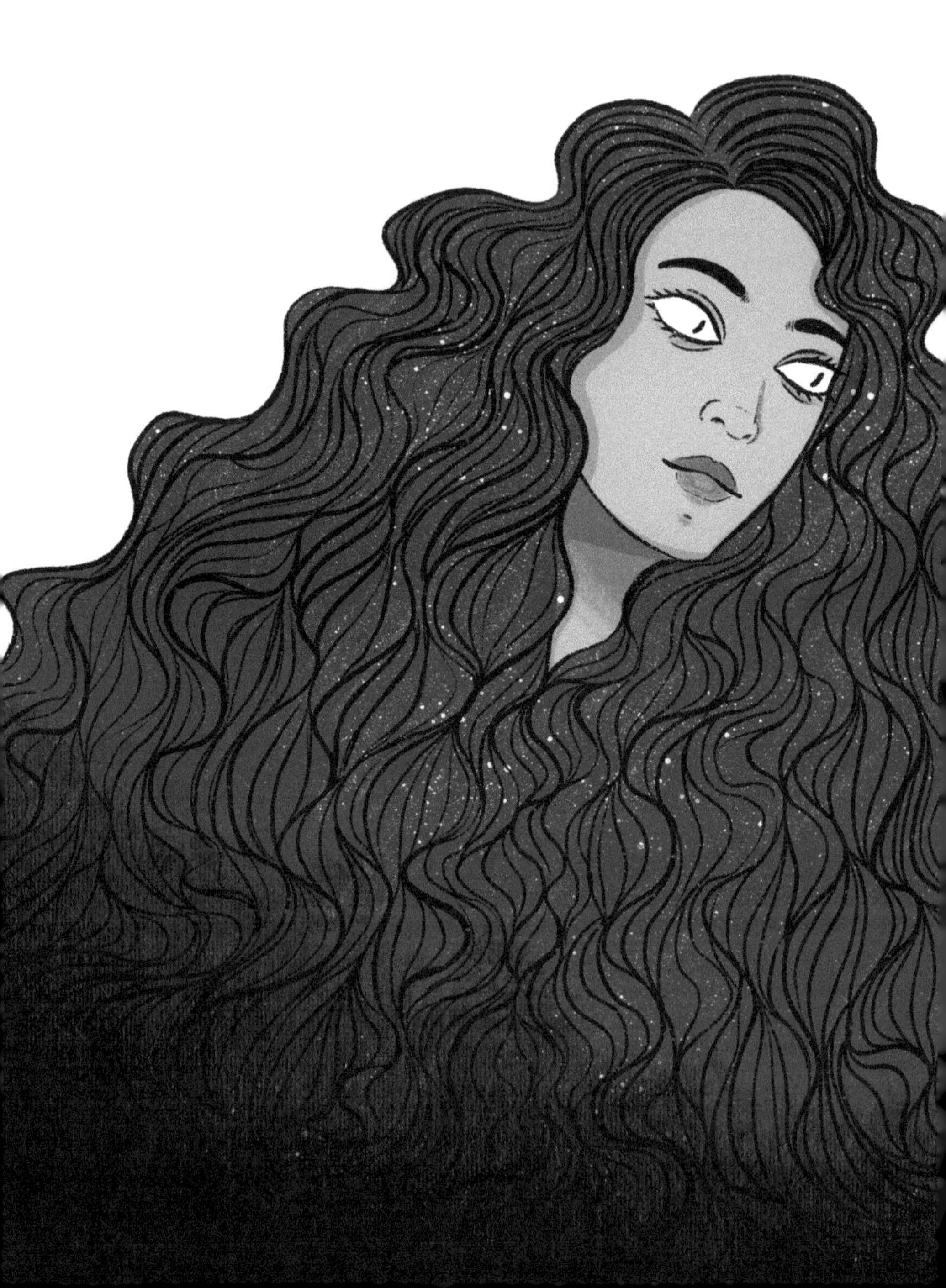

if grief were a person
i'd be hers
and she'd be mine
we'd drown in each other
and we'd be fine.

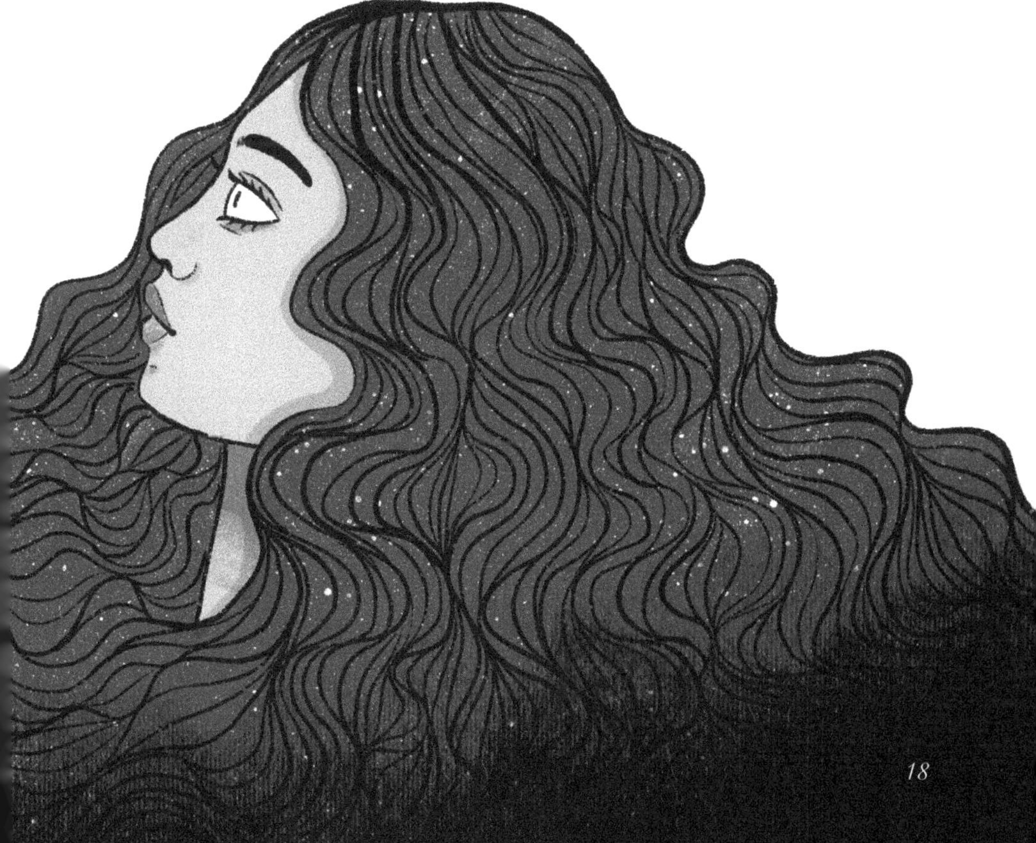

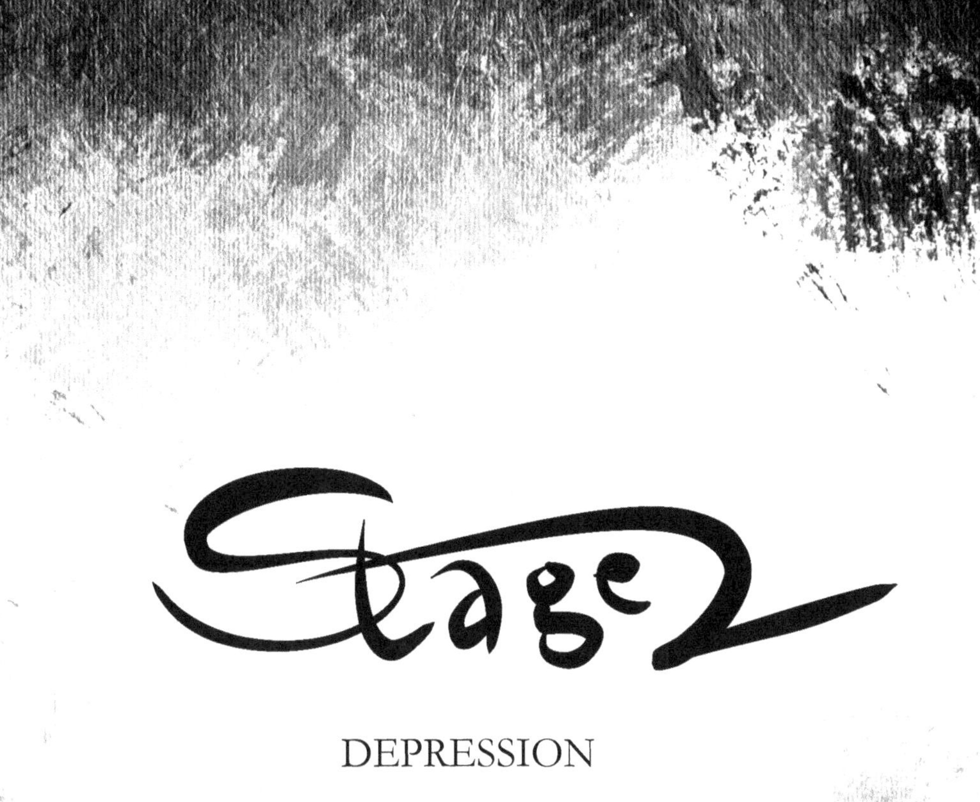

Stage 2

DEPRESSION

— so, she didn't really die and now she's sad —

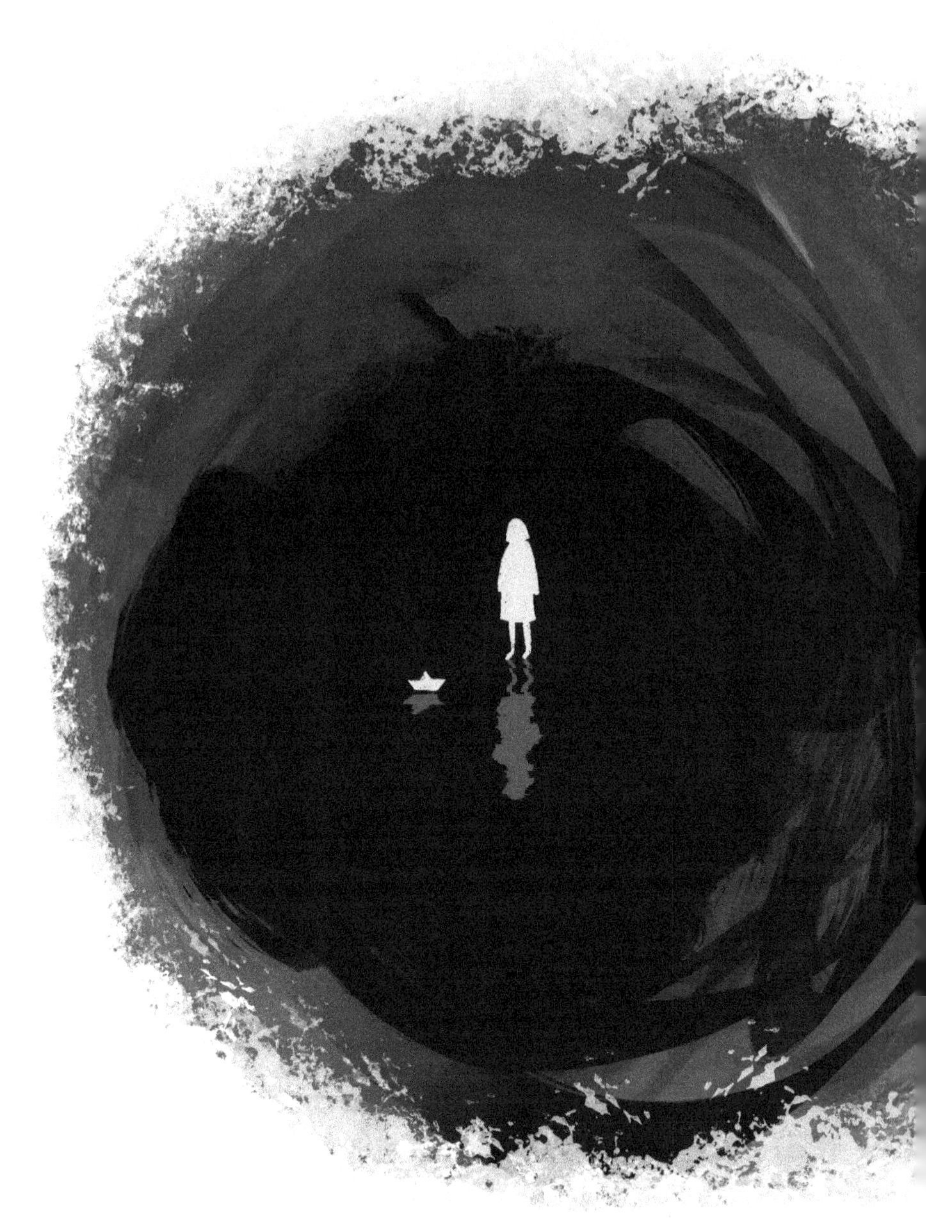

*N*ow drown

why try so hard to stay afloat?
why not stab a hole in this boat?

it's already going down
and down
why not drown?
now drown

sinking low
into the bottomless dark
when it all ends,
will there be peace at last?

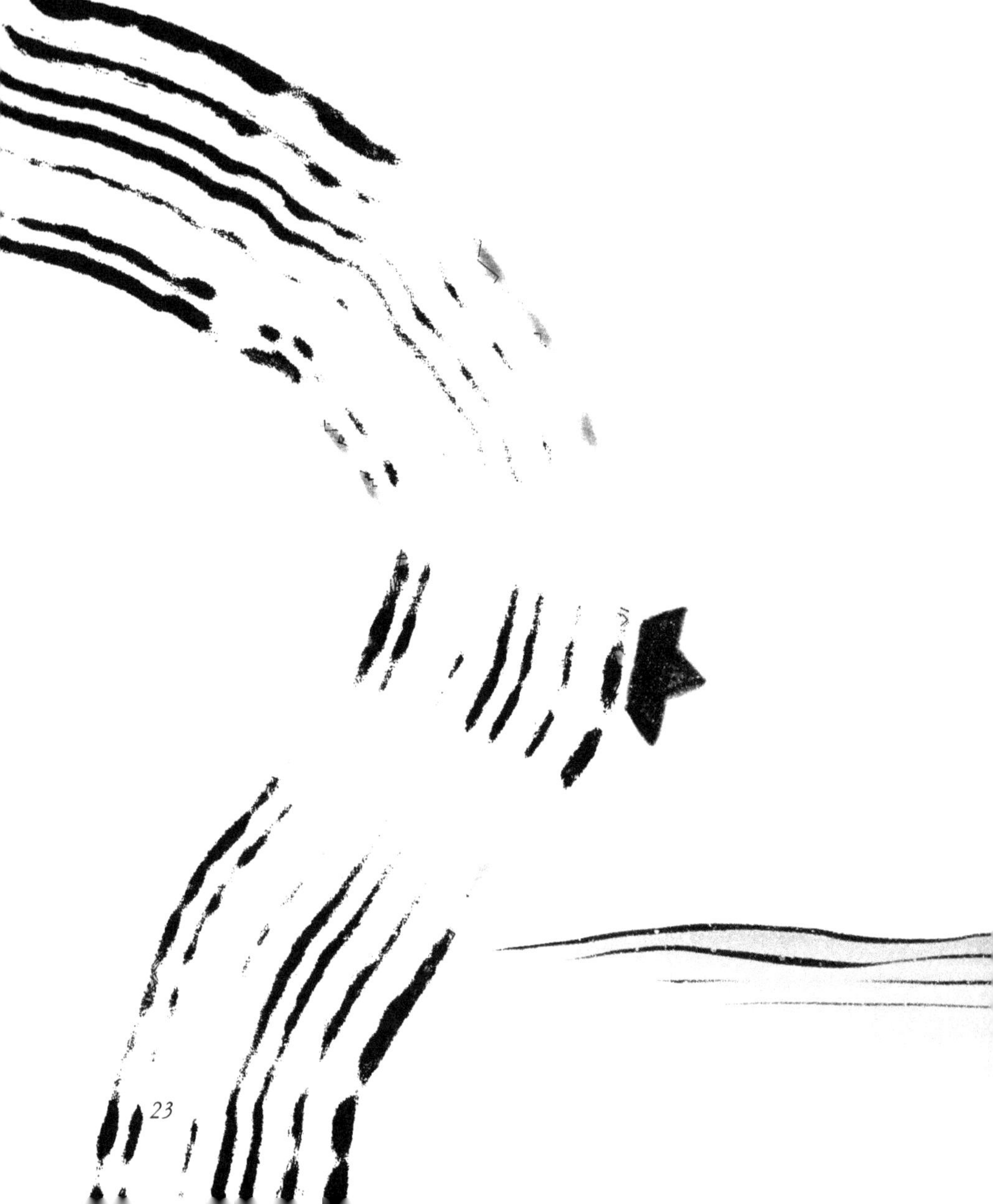

23

why try so hard to stay afloat?
they already made holes in this boat

it's going down
just drown
now drown.

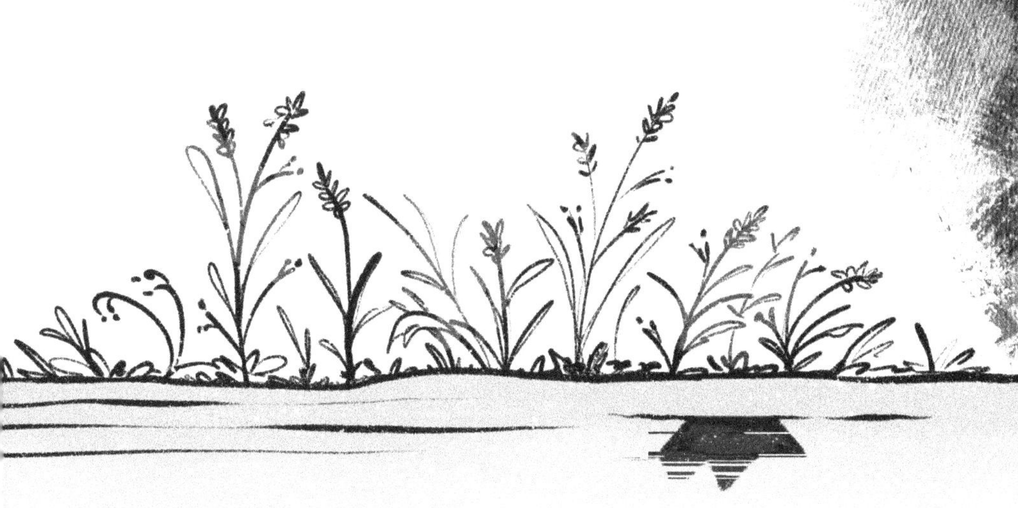

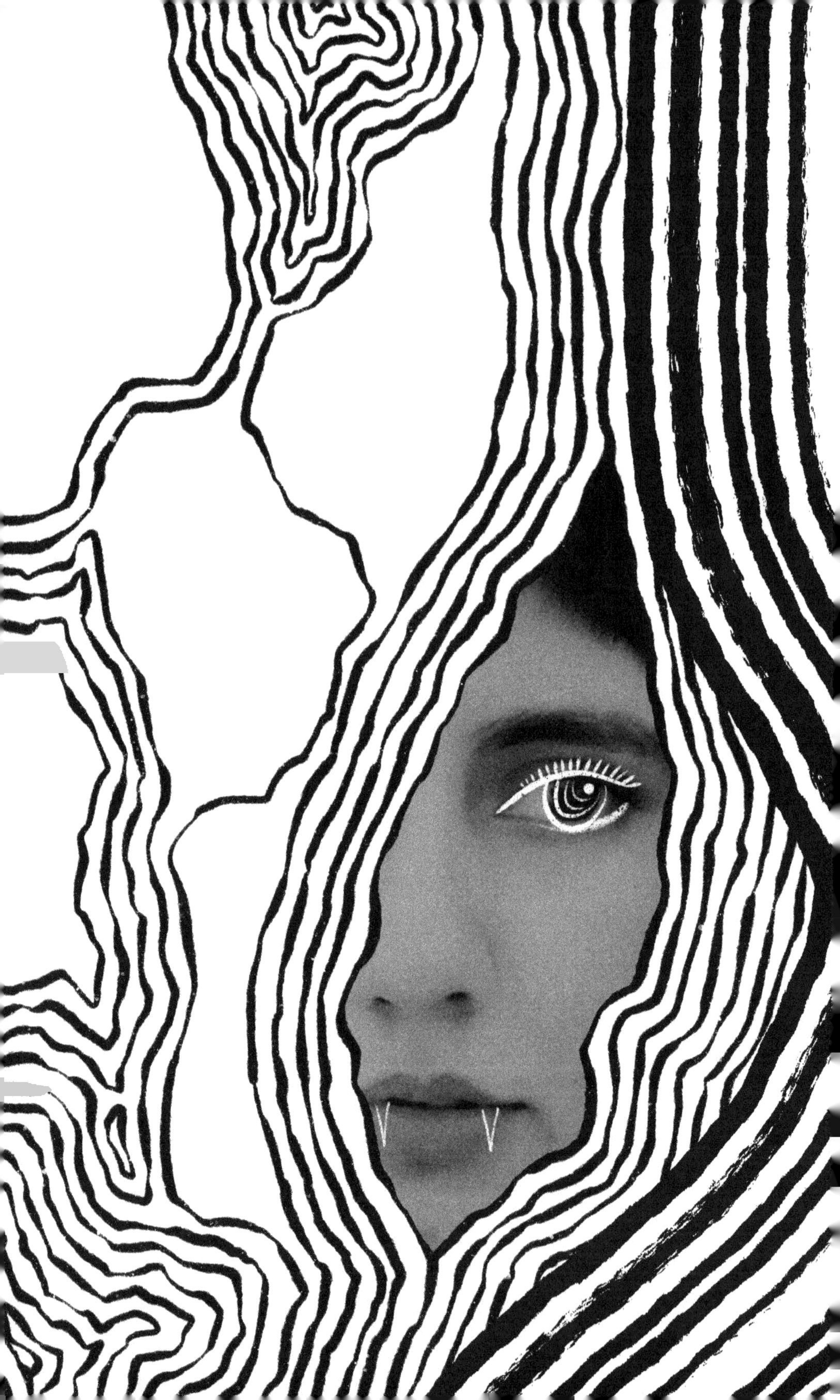

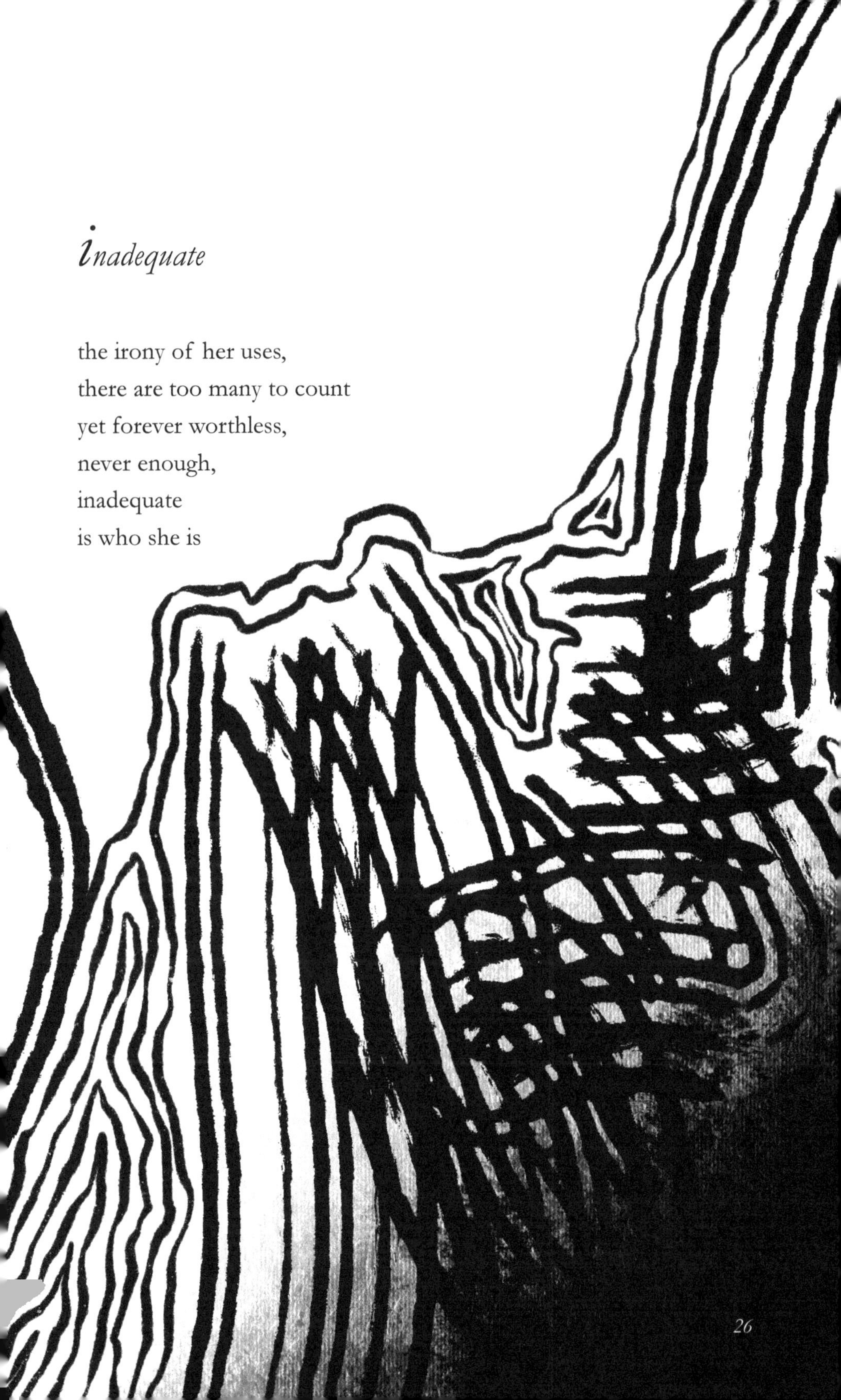

*i*nadequate

the irony of her uses,
there are too many to count
yet forever worthless,
never enough,
inadequate
is who she is

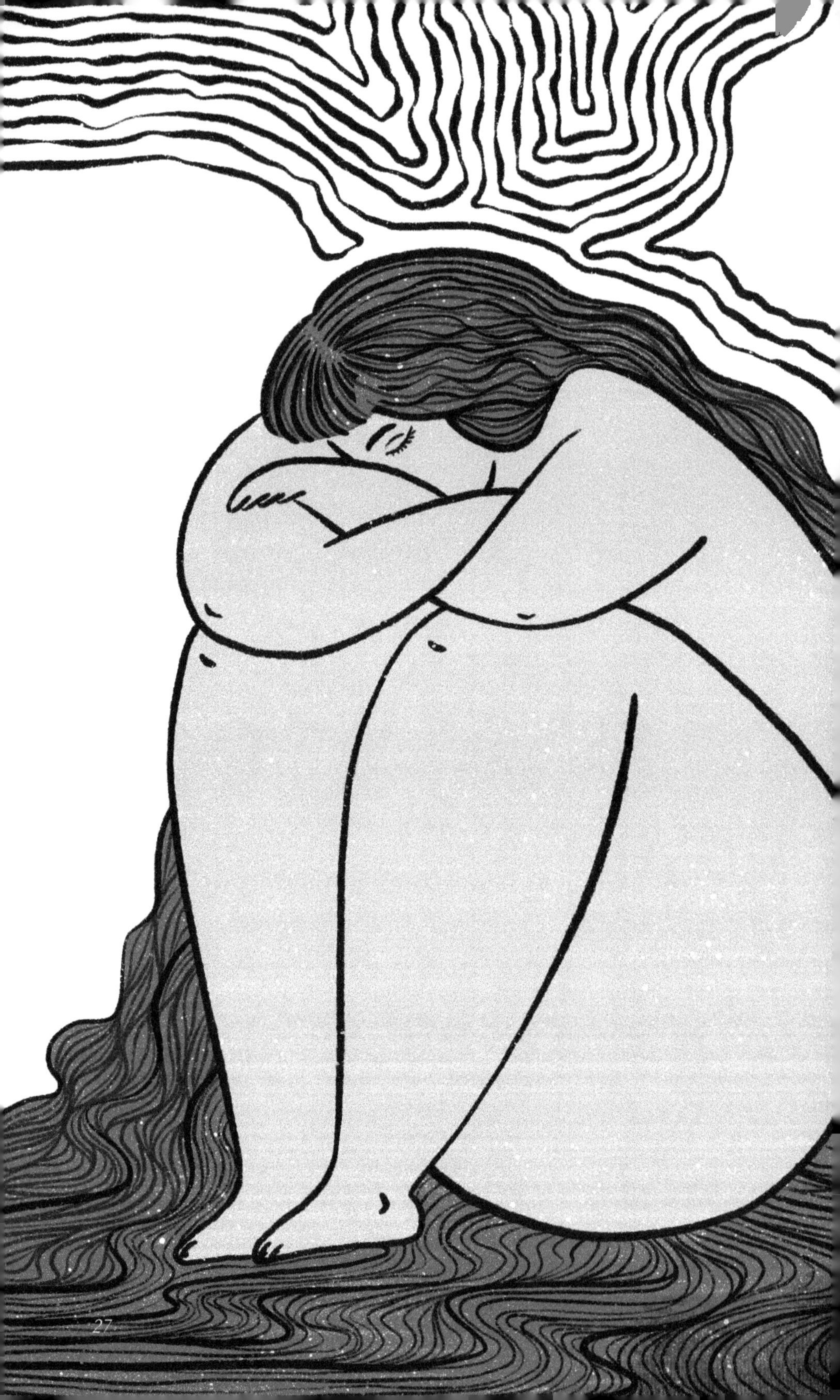

she is also, however,
a monster, so clever,
so hideous, she better hide
an inconvenience, she is much too wide

needed, she isn't wanted at all
a dated porcelain doll
wrung out, too small
she is inadequate, that's all.

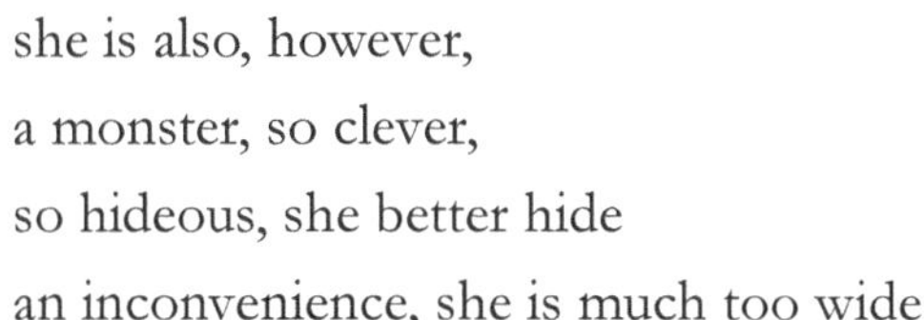

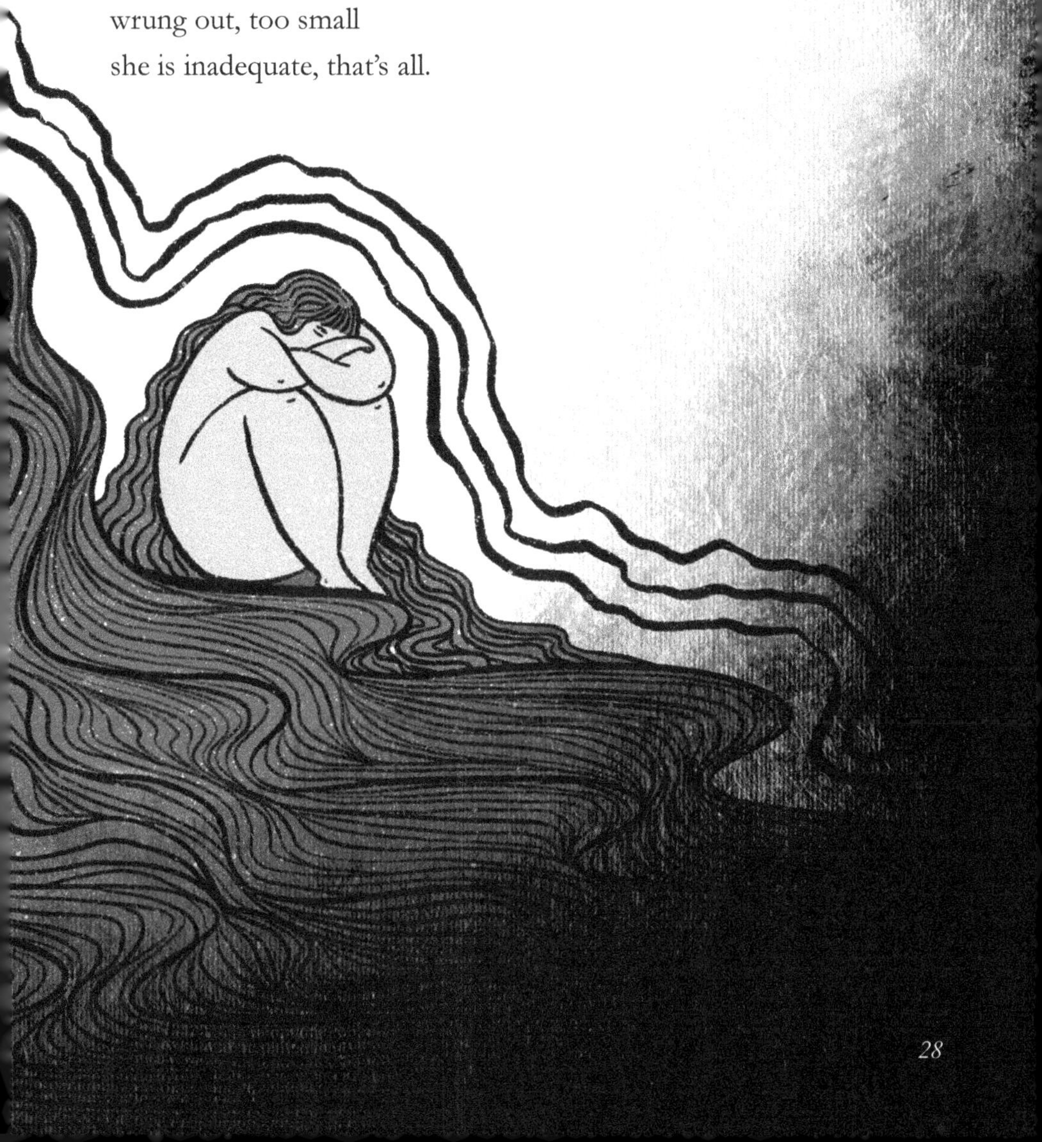

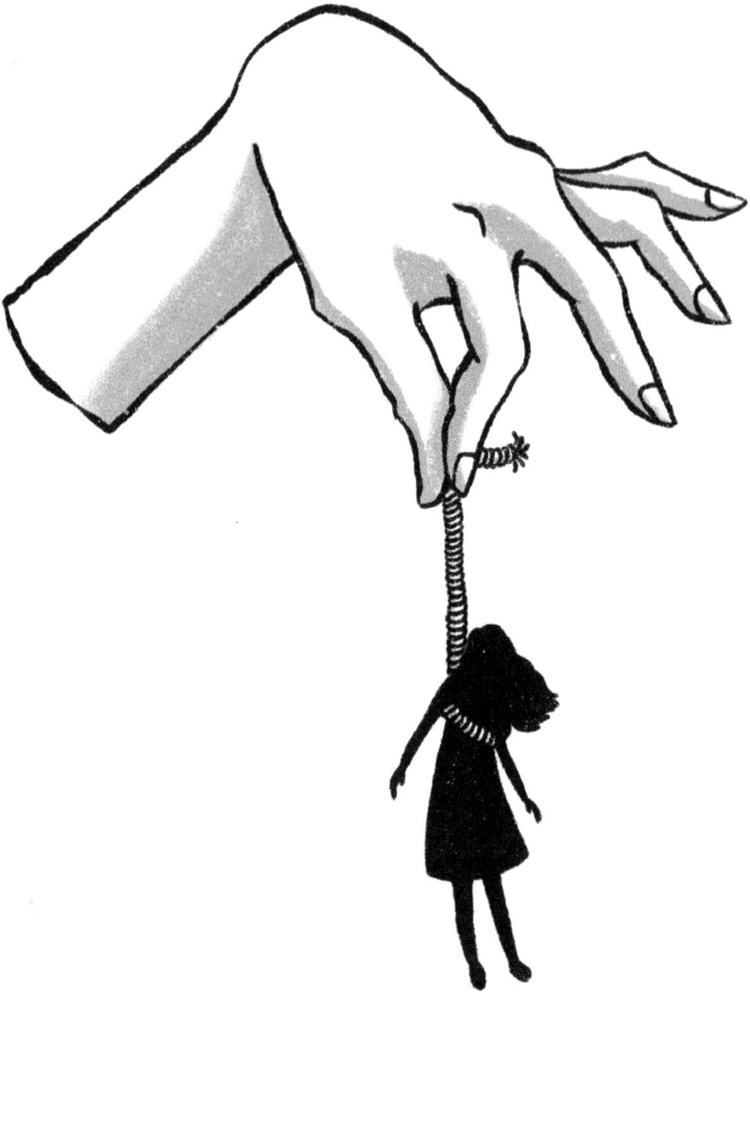

*i*deation

some days she marches just a foot ahead, stalked
others, she's the stalker
some nights you lurk in the shadows of her light
others, she sits snug in your lap
considering the embrace
maybe merging wouldn't be so bad

after all, you've been her only constant
in the transience of everything
for too long, far too long
she's been stretching herself thin

should she wipe the slate clean,
take your hand?
would it hurt
if she lets snap the rubber band?

will there be peace in the aftermath,
quiet at last?
grief won't be hers anymore,
future nor past

ideation dear,
you haven't been fleeting at all
coaxing her to stay down
at every trip, after every fall

you don't come and go
you came, and you stayed
or maybe you were born the day she was
or maybe you followed from a lifetime past

did she lean into the temptation
of your arms back then?
will the cycle repeat
if she gives in once again?

the game looping back
to start over
of the eternally stalked
and the stalker

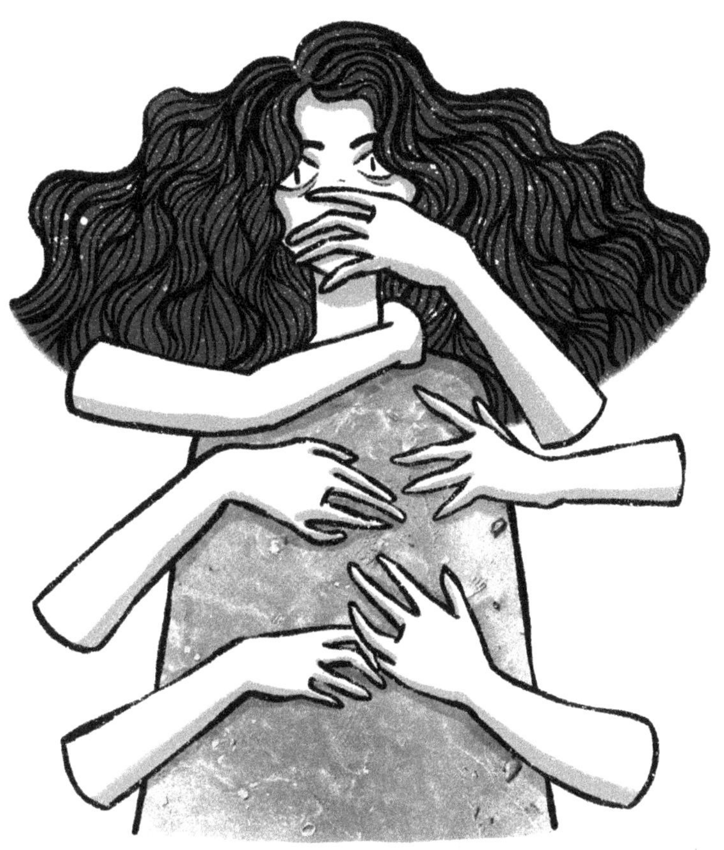

you're already hers
so maybe sit for a while
she might let you
starve this time

for you have been
and you will be
there will always be tomorrow
for her to give in.

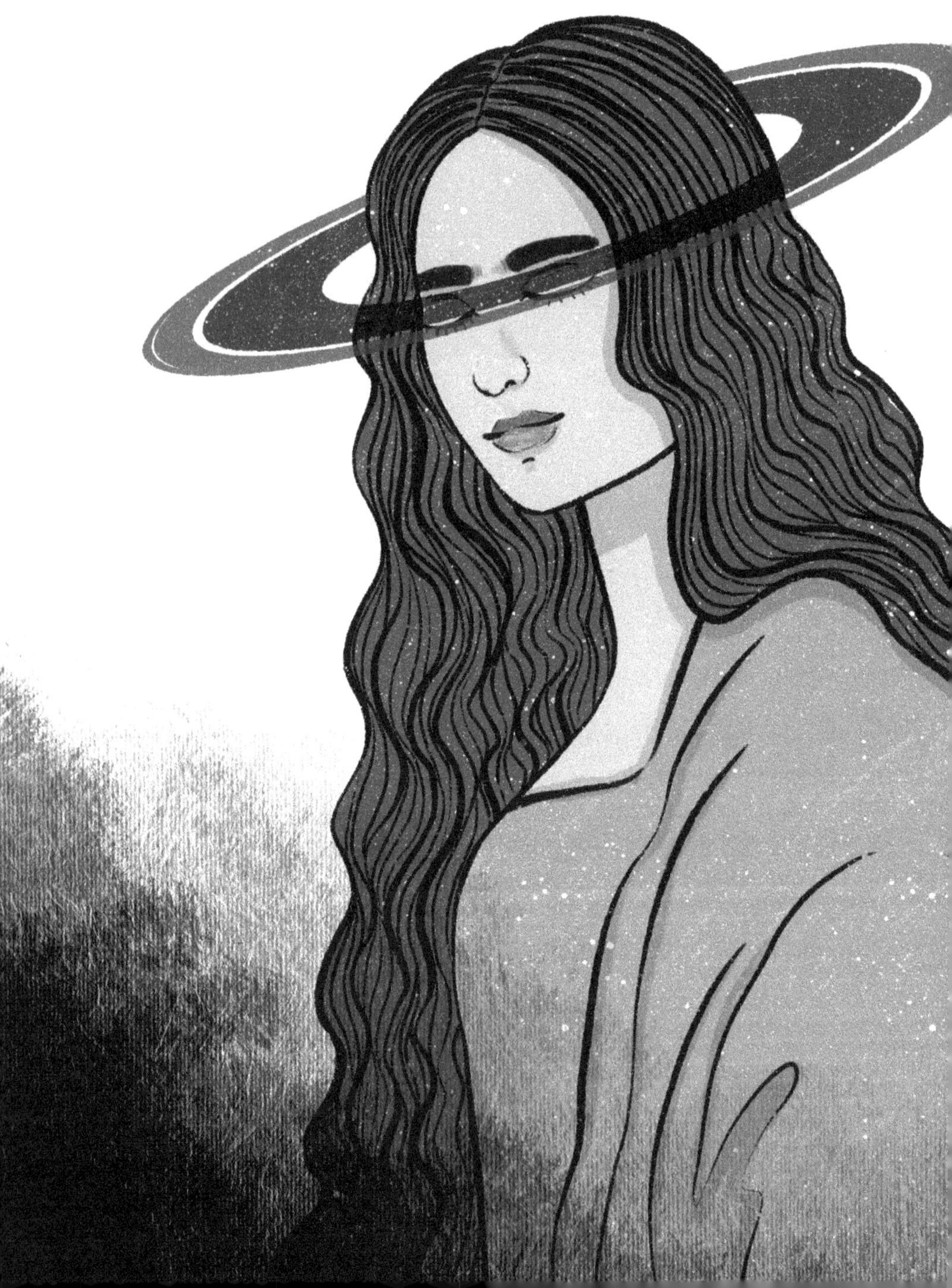

resilience

what do you want her to do with the resilience,
when a semicolon ends her every sentence?
what do you want her to do with her edges,
and her snaking walls and concrete grudges?

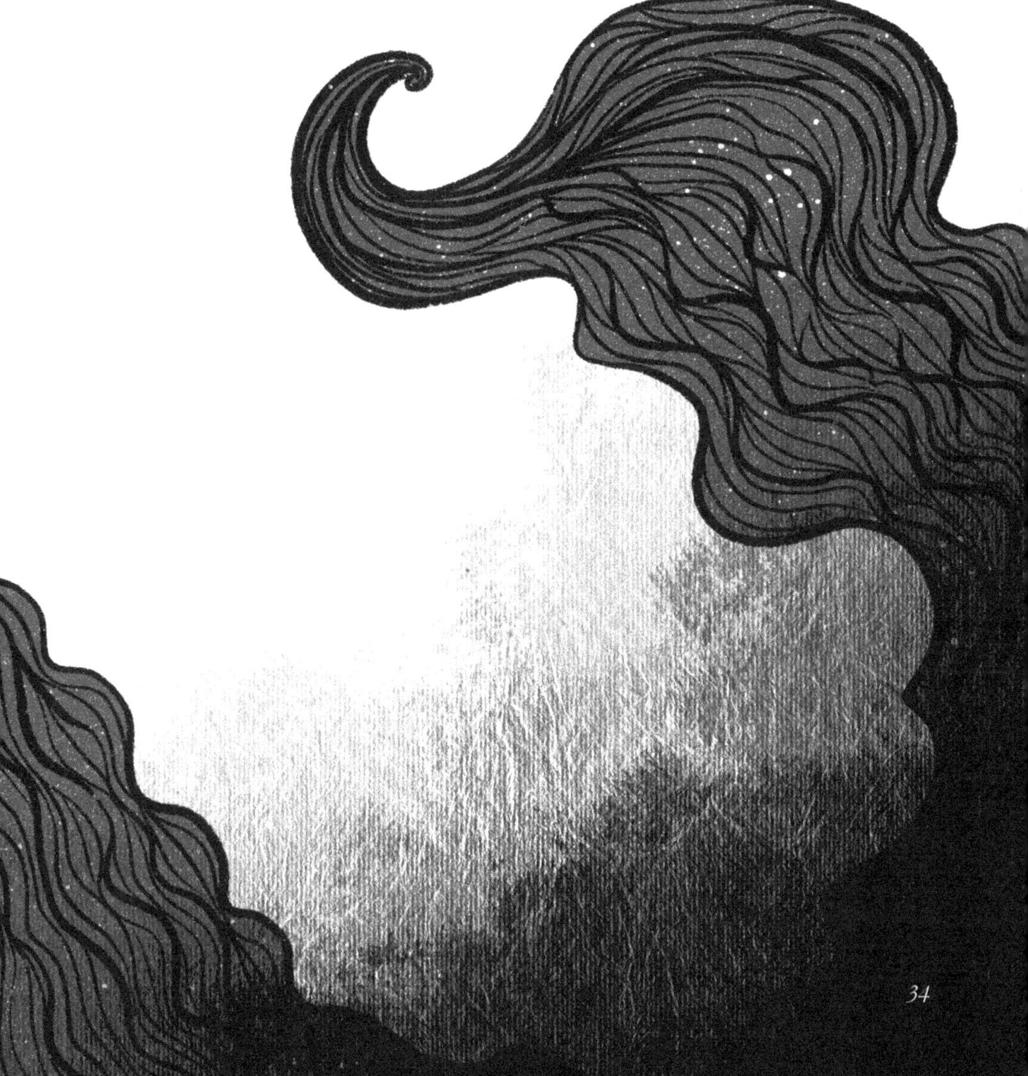

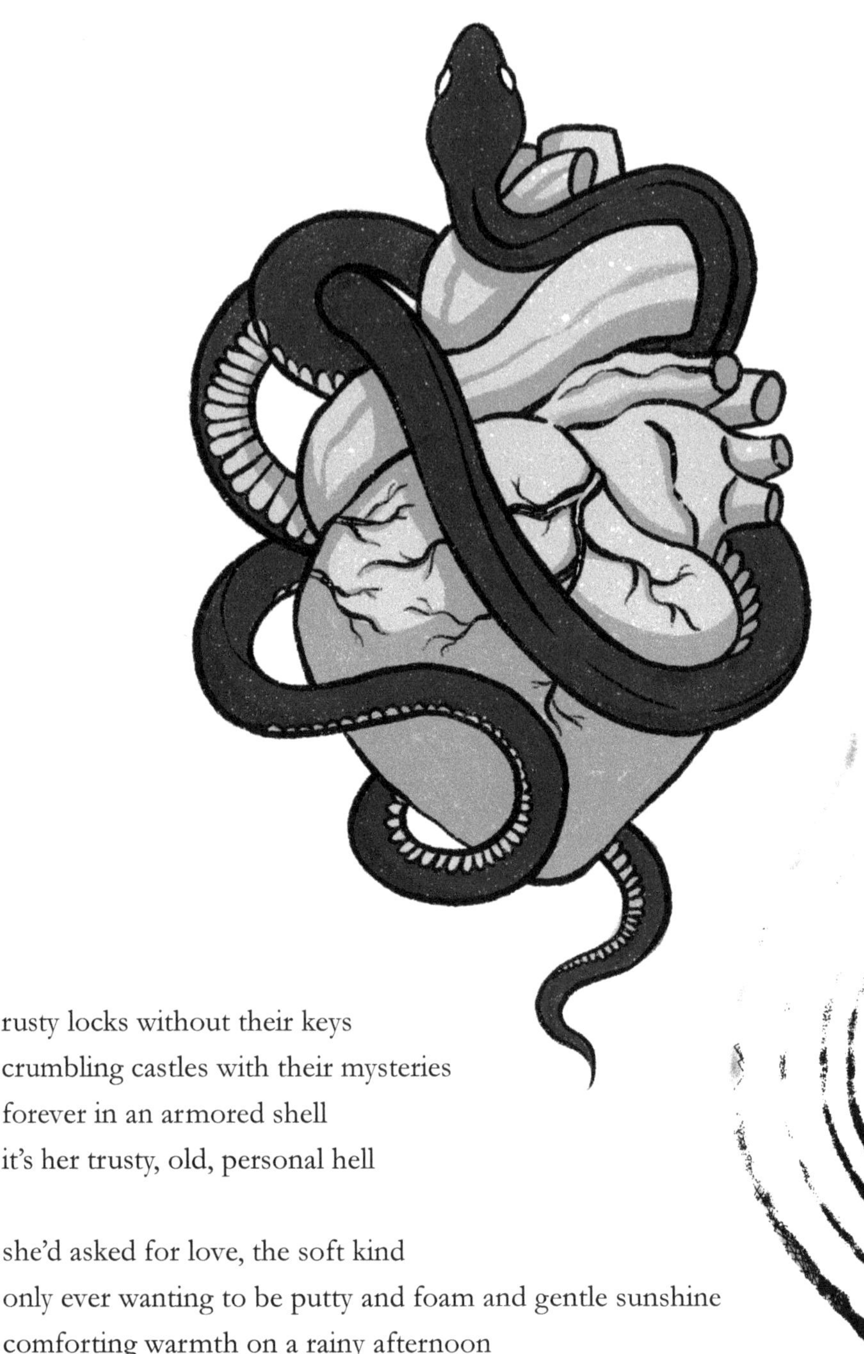

rusty locks without their keys
crumbling castles with their mysteries
forever in an armored shell
it's her trusty, old, personal hell

she'd asked for love, the soft kind
only ever wanting to be putty and foam and gentle sunshine
comforting warmth on a rainy afternoon
the fuzzy haze around a happy moon

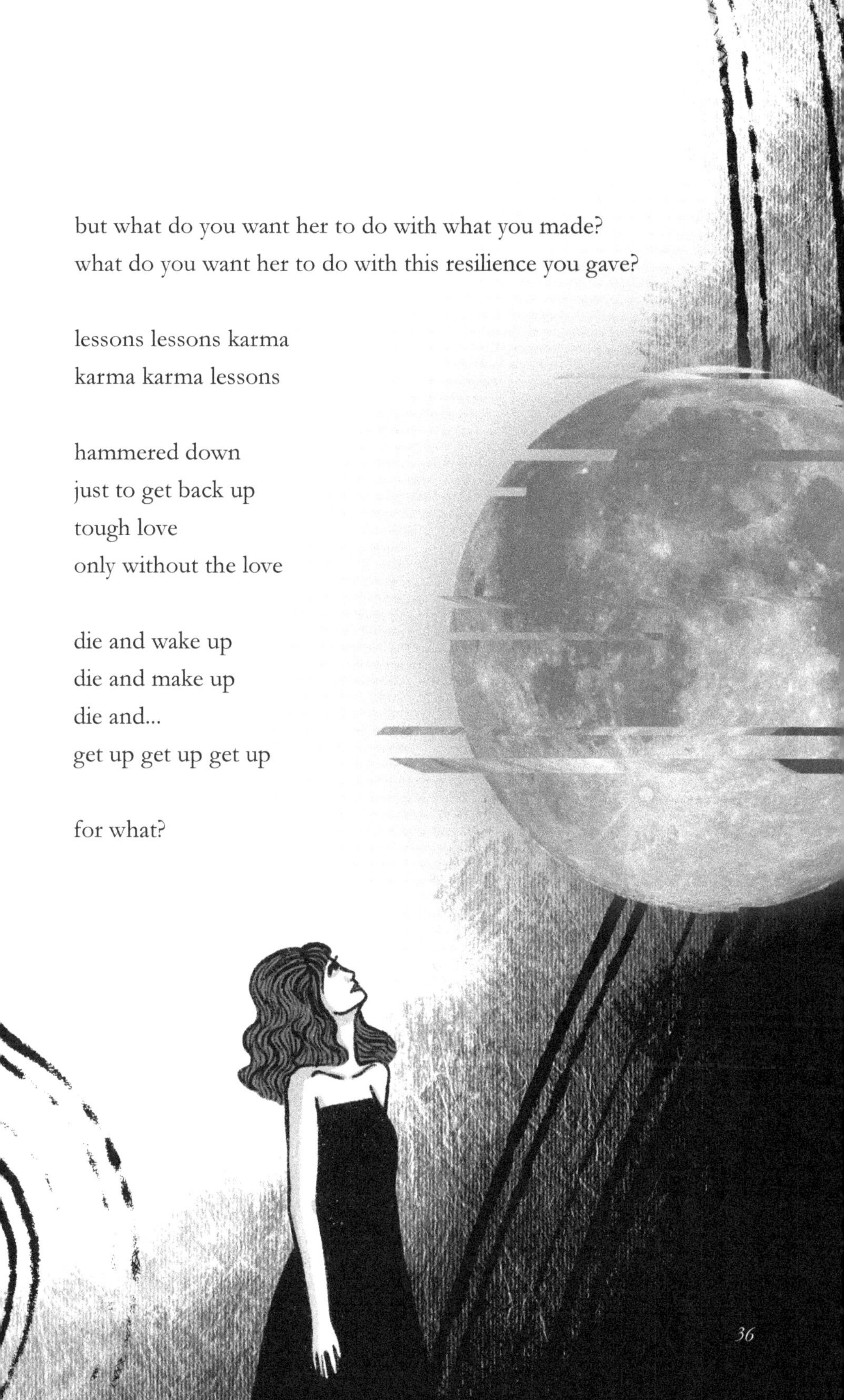

but what do you want her to do with what you made?
what do you want her to do with this resilience you gave?

lessons lessons karma
karma karma lessons

hammered down
just to get back up
tough love
only without the love

die and wake up
die and make up
die and...
get up get up get up

for what?

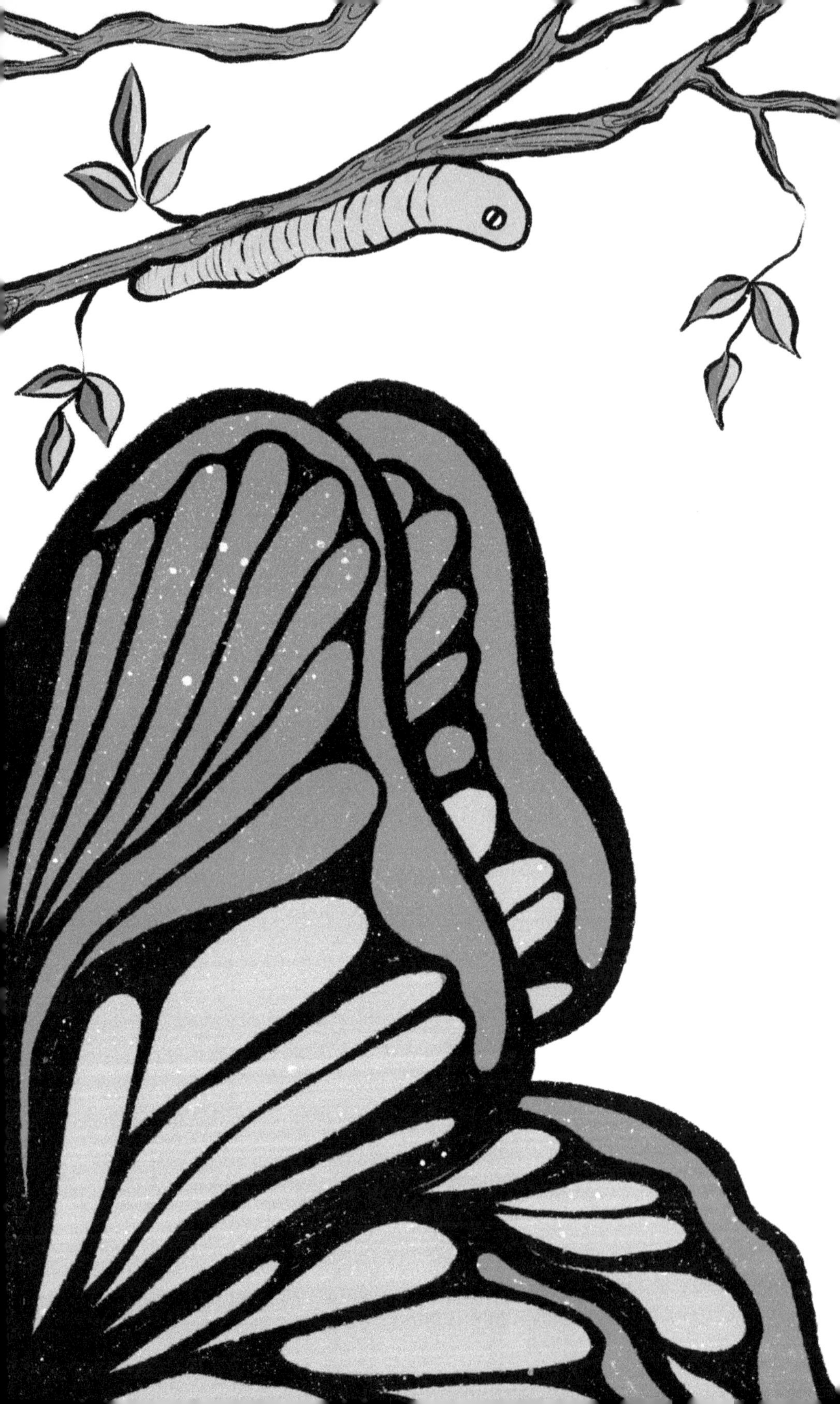

Cocoon

her skin crawls, too warm
but the bones froze a long time ago
or maybe they never knew warmth
she wouldn't know

she shudders, on fire again
is it hot or cold, embers or chills
is this smoke or a catastrophic mist
maybe she's too soft for this

"worm, you'll be a butterfly soon"
but she doesn't even have a cocoon

don't look at her, she no longer cares
she stopped holding truths or playing dares
the game was always rigged for Schrödinger's cat
retired with merit as Skinner's former rat

she's too far gone
too much too less
from the hot and cold
it's always somebody else's mess

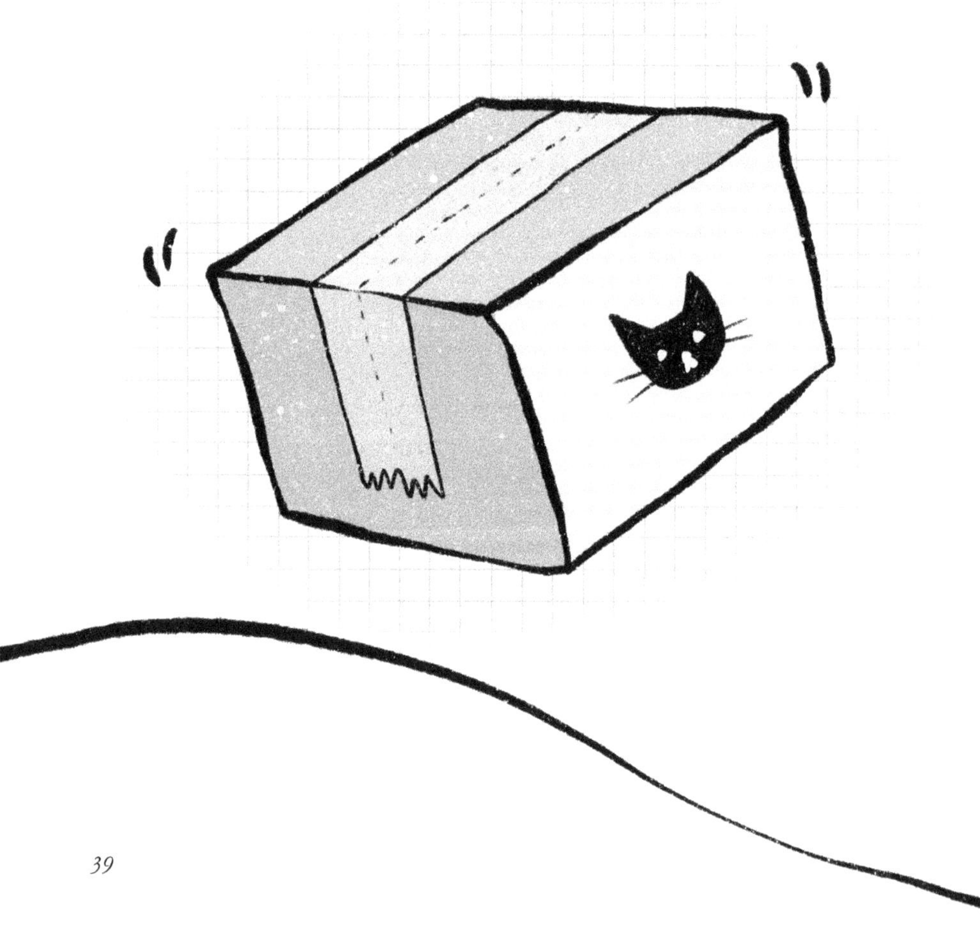

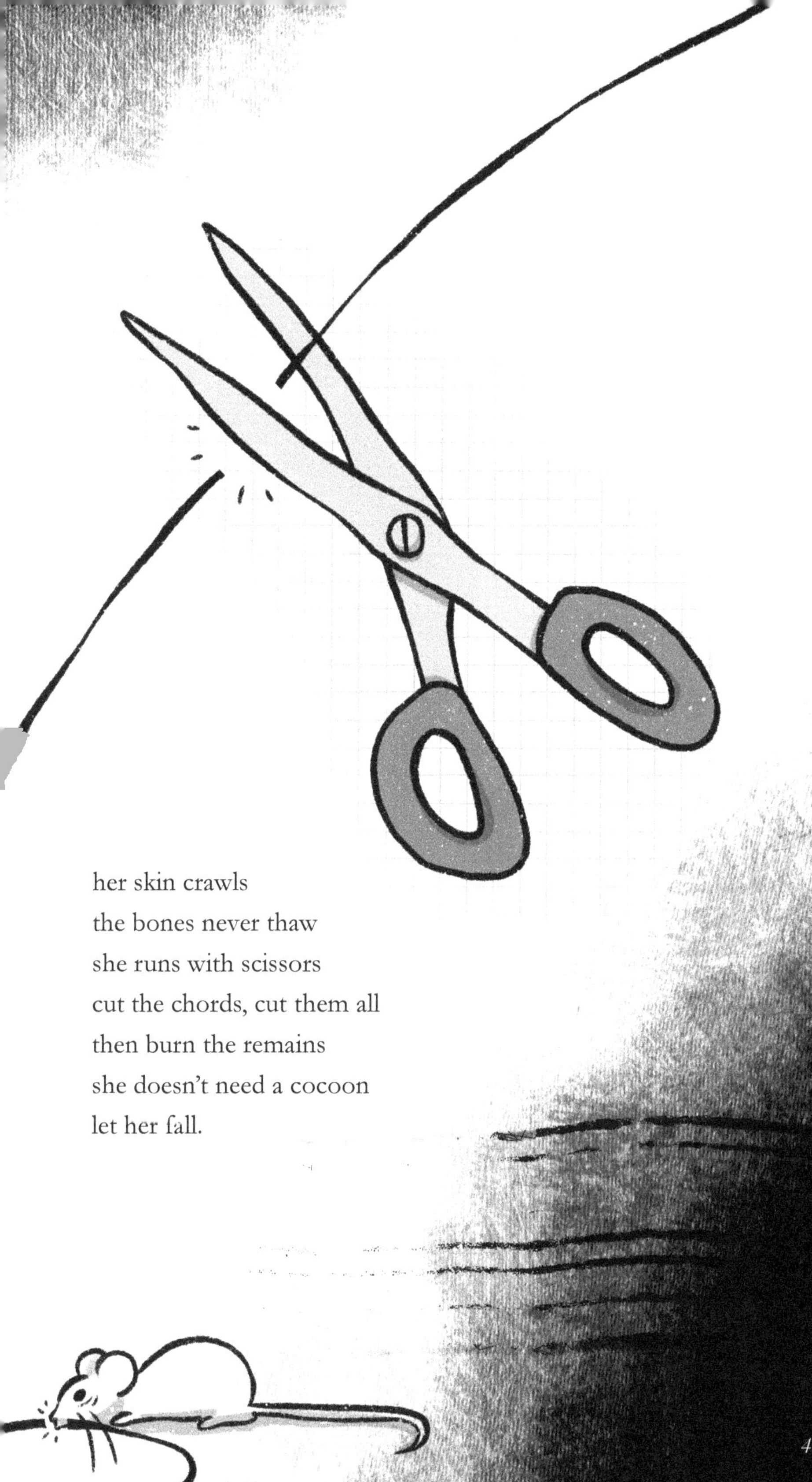

her skin crawls
the bones never thaw
she runs with scissors
cut the chords, cut them all
then burn the remains
she doesn't need a cocoon
let her fall.

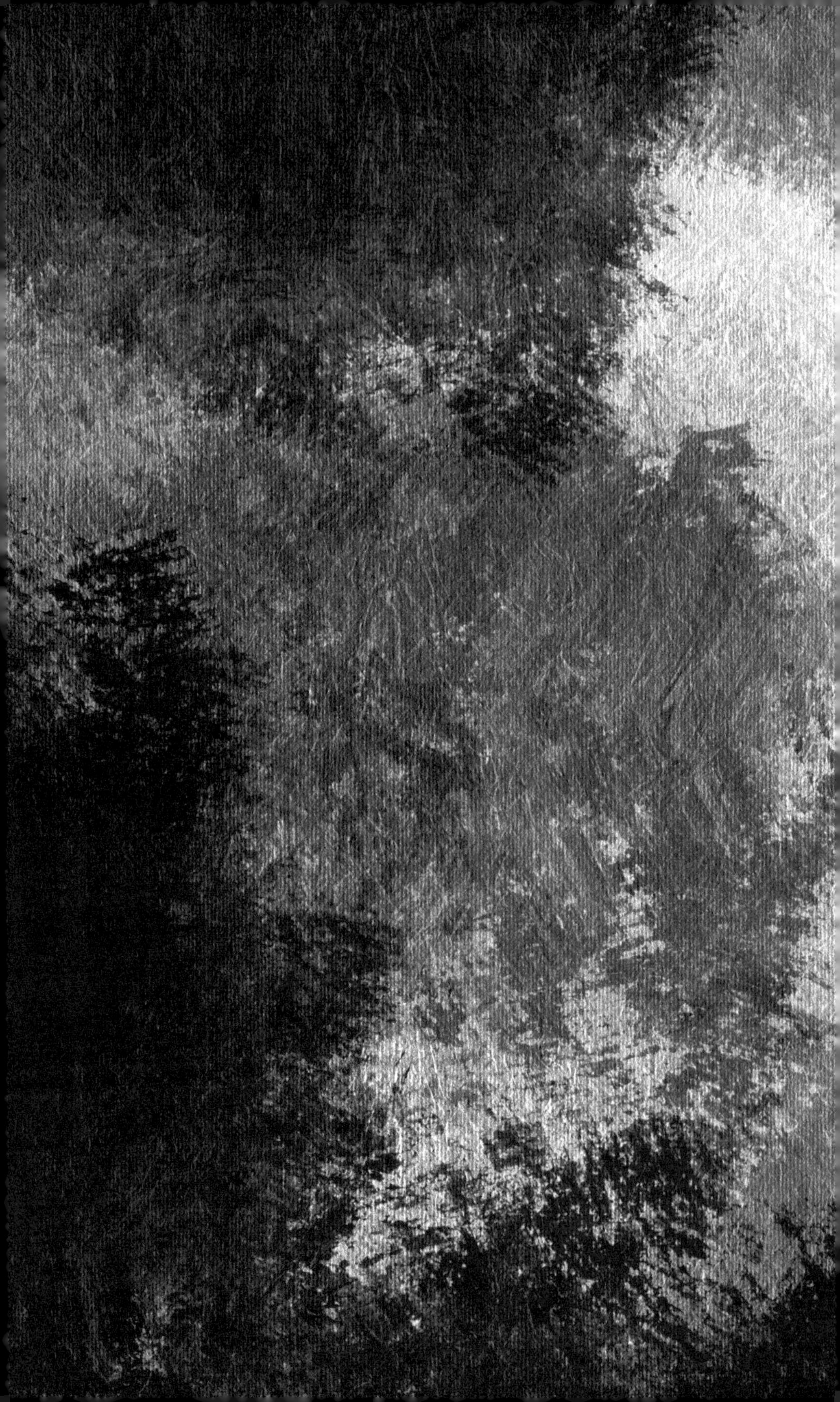

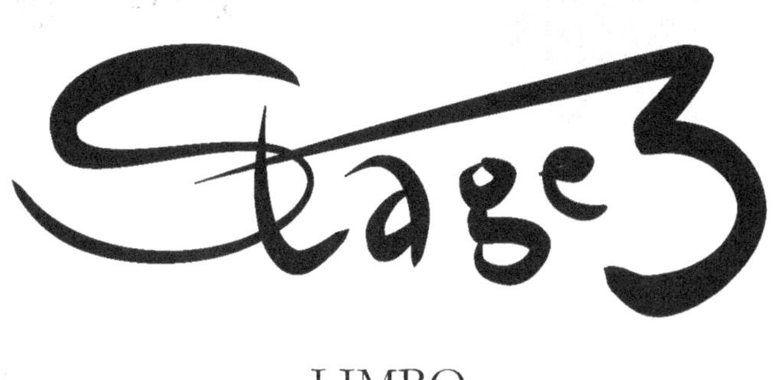

LIMBO

— is it really okay to cry? —

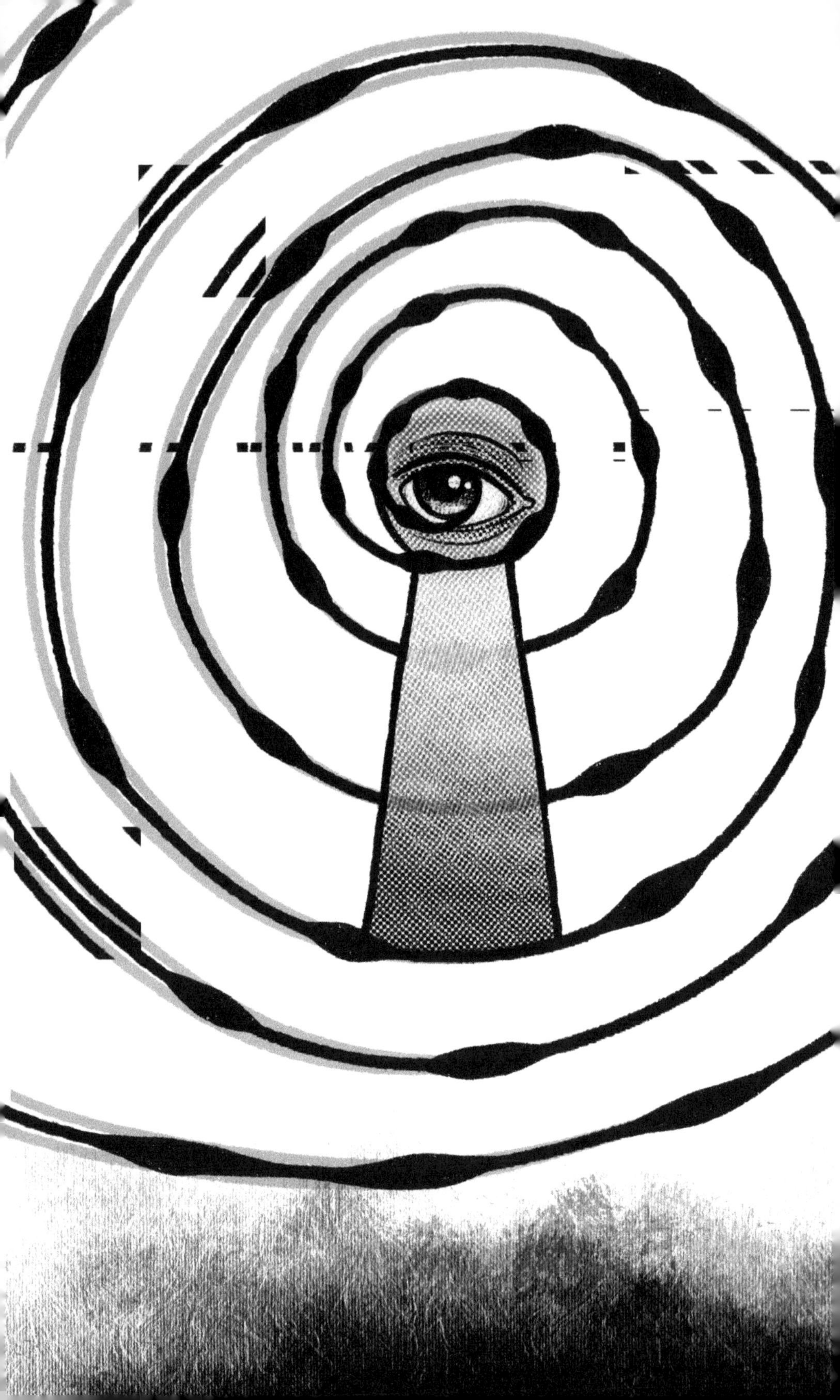

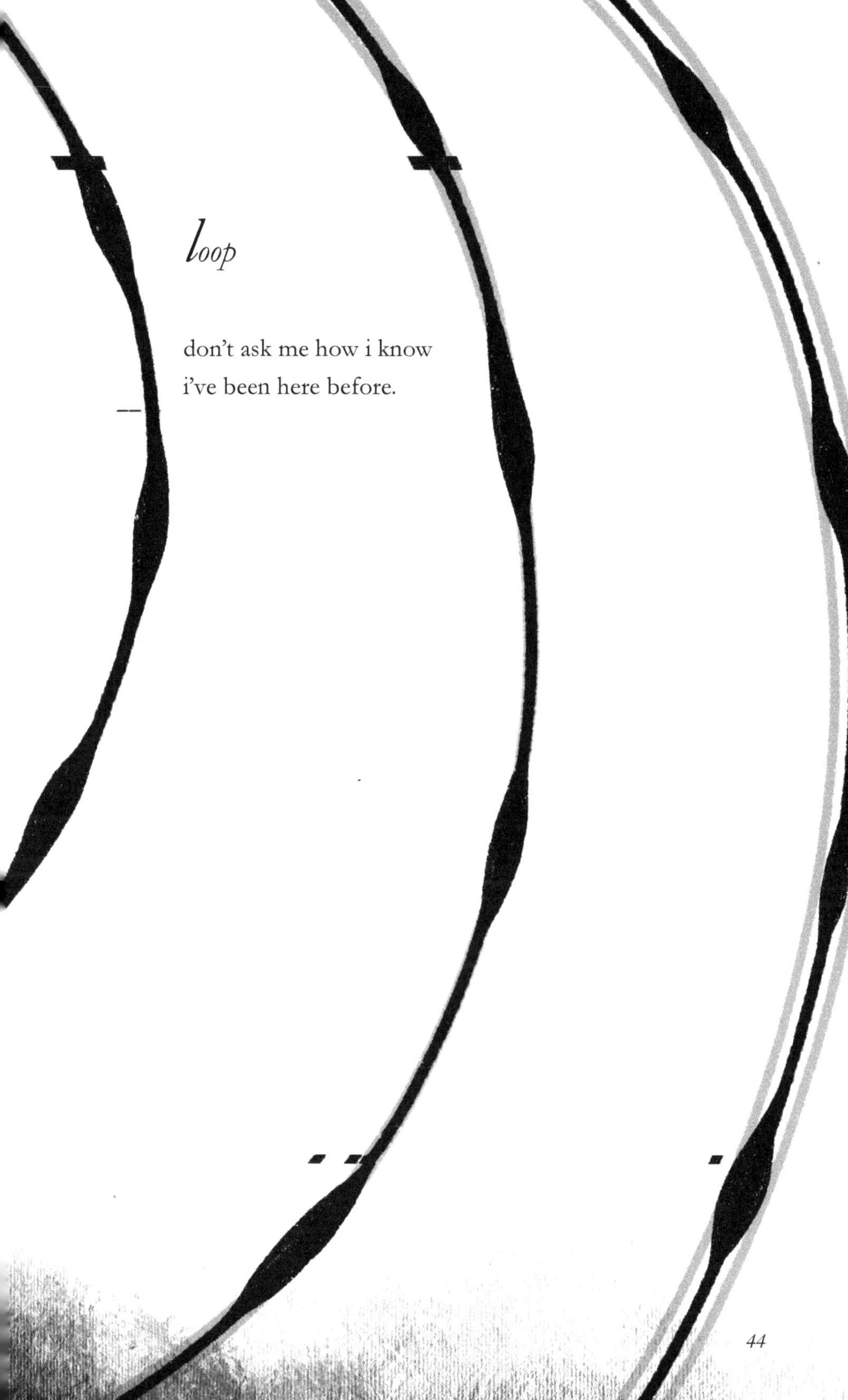

loop

don't ask me how i know
i've been here before.

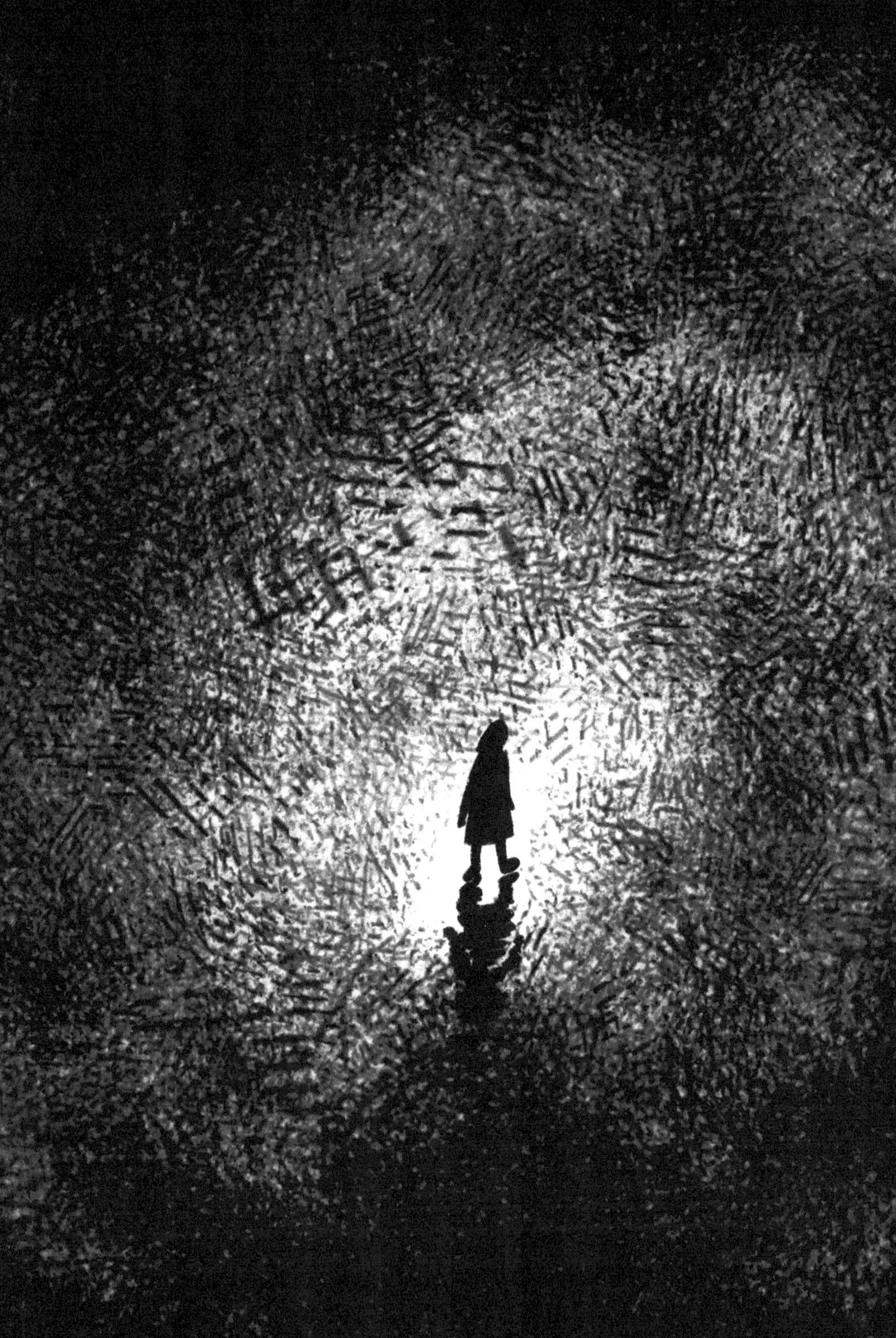

*f*eel

she lived in a world
wading through a sea of people
trying not to feel
it was too much sometimes
too much for her skin
too much for her bones
too much for her soul

she lived in a world
wading through a sea of people
numbing herself
numbing it all
till she forgot how to feel
everything, anything, nothing
even a little bit, at all

and now she's living in a world
wading through a sea of people
it is still too much... sometimes
more than most times
but she's learning again
learning to feel something
and nothing and everything

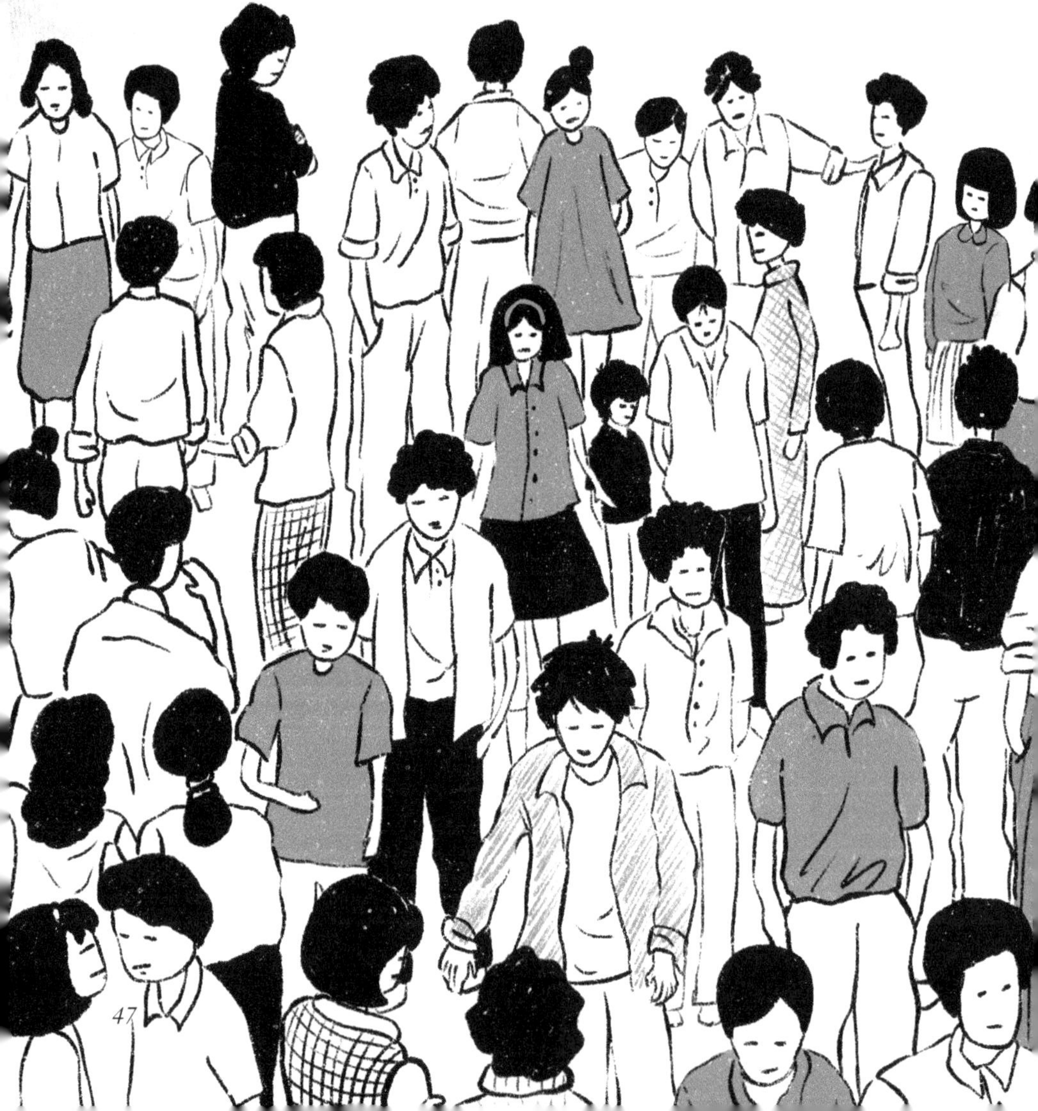

she wasn't meant to remember too soon
but she was here
you were here
we were here all along

she lives in a world
we live in a world
wading through a sea of people
and we're all trying to feel
we're all trying to feel something.

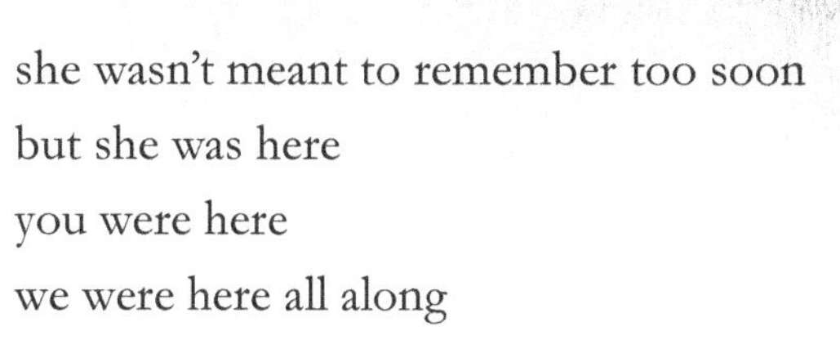

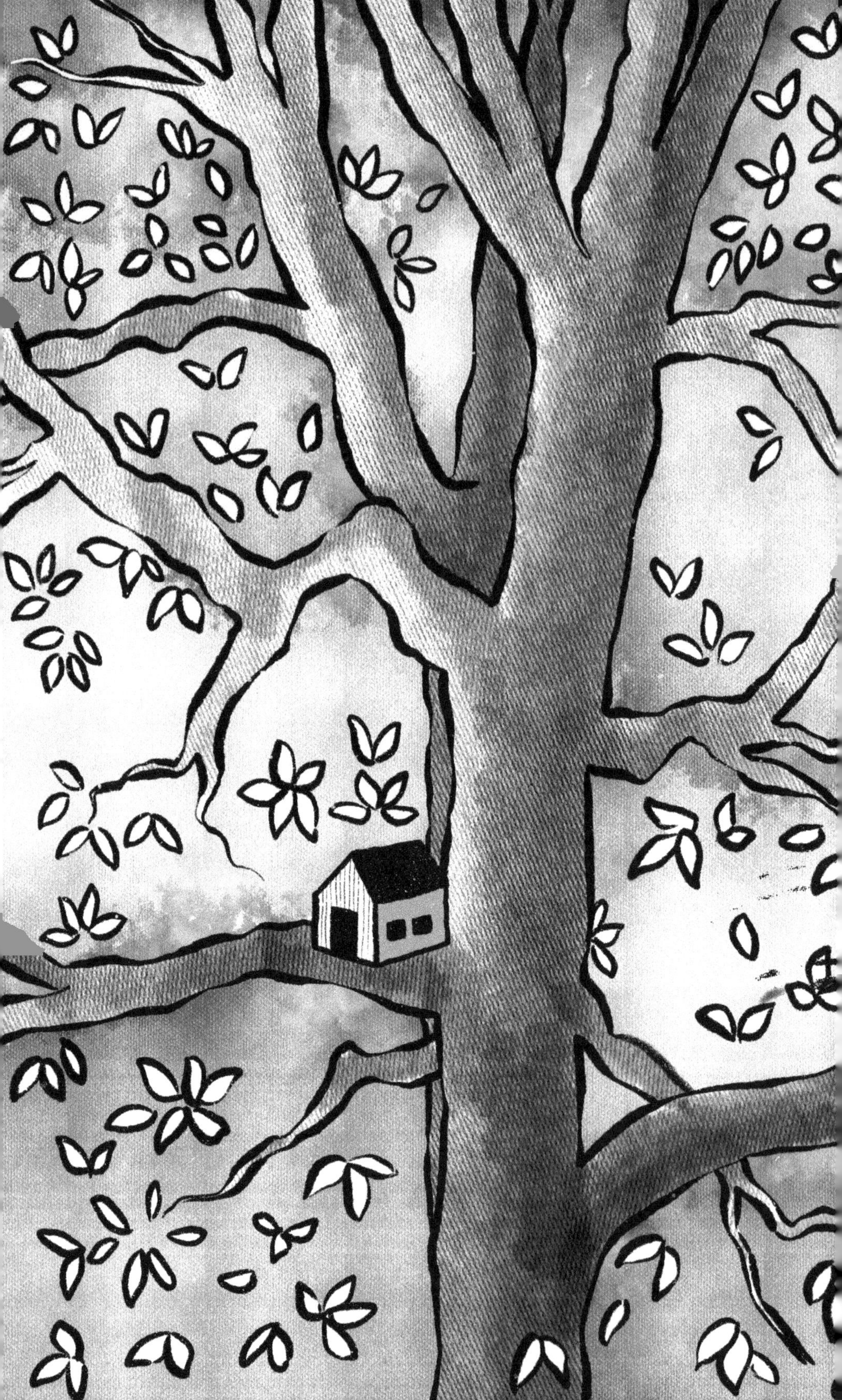

Addictive

close your eyes and see
just how addictive it is
this solitude
this love of isolation
in her one-woman nation

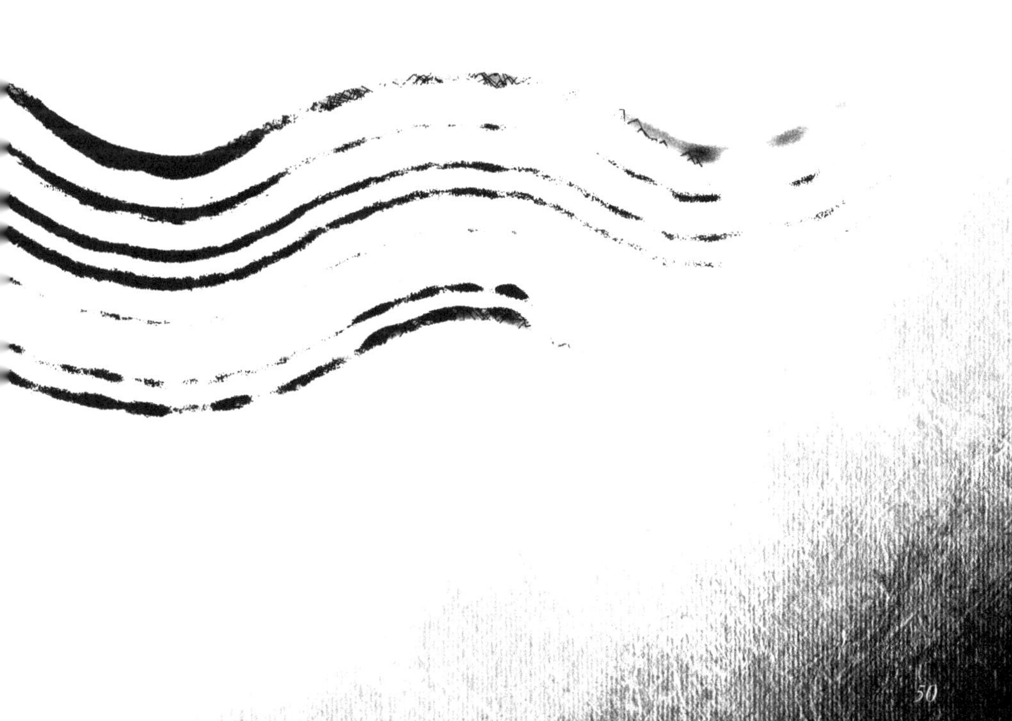

it might seem hard from afar
from where you are
but once you've tasted it
the elixir of peace
the absolute ease
this love of isolation
in her one-woman nation

you don't ever want to go back
it's just you and your purring cat
there's music, there's art
spring sunshine, and your new guitar

it's addictive, this solitude
fair warning: there is no cure
nor antidote
you're a hermit in love
touch it once
and it's yours

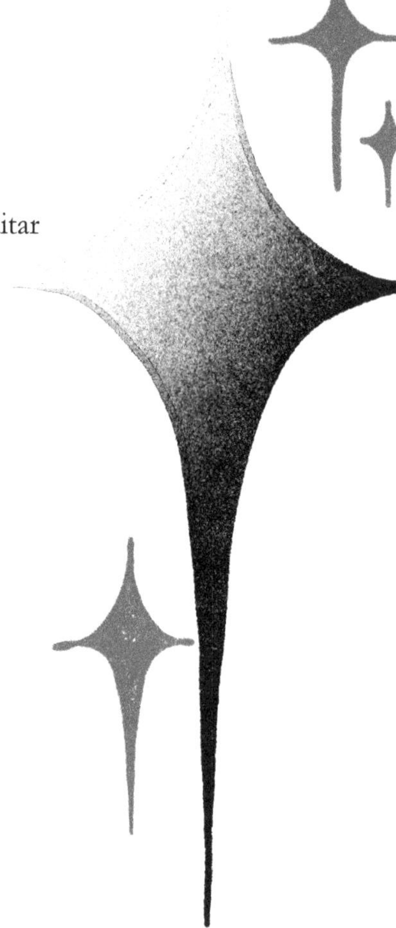

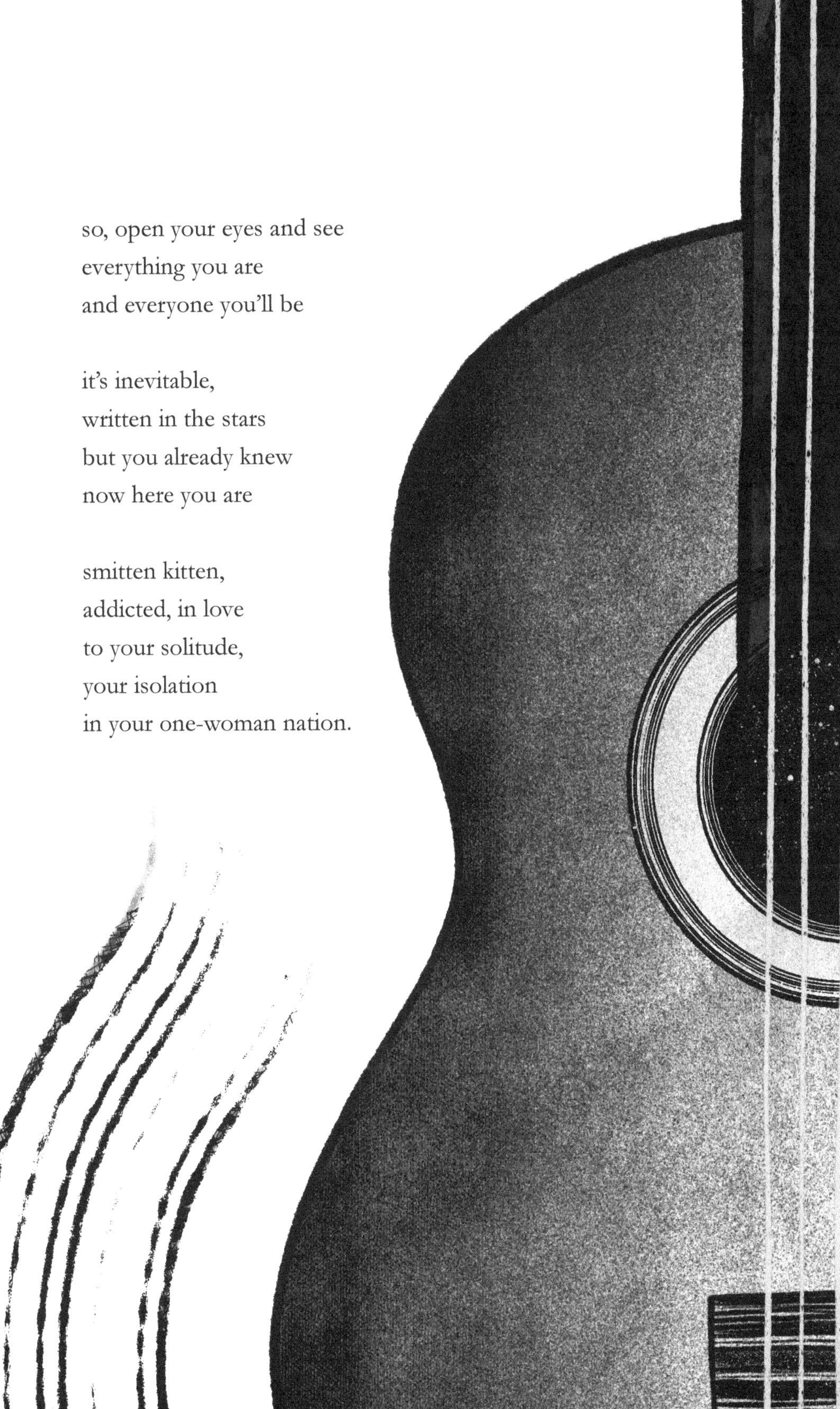

so, open your eyes and see
everything you are
and everyone you'll be

it's inevitable,
written in the stars
but you already knew
now here you are

smitten kitten,
addicted, in love
to your solitude,
your isolation
in your one-woman nation.

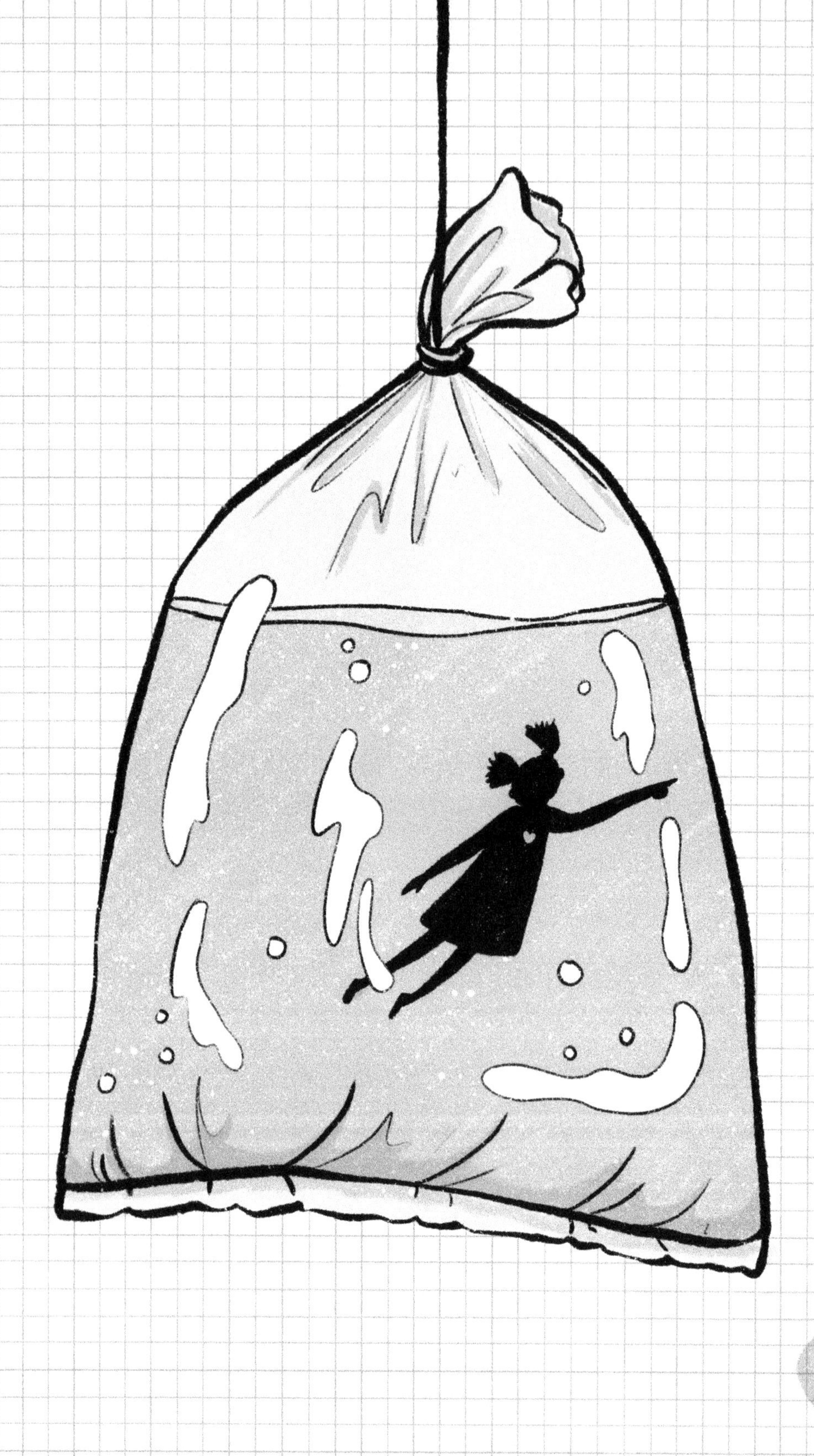

What now?

you scroll through the contacts
there's no one to call
stare blankly at the screen
try not to fling it at a wall

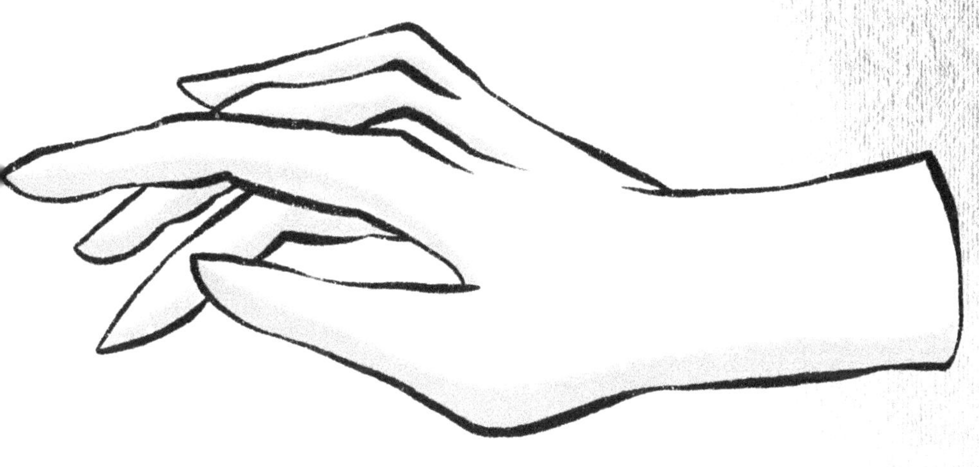

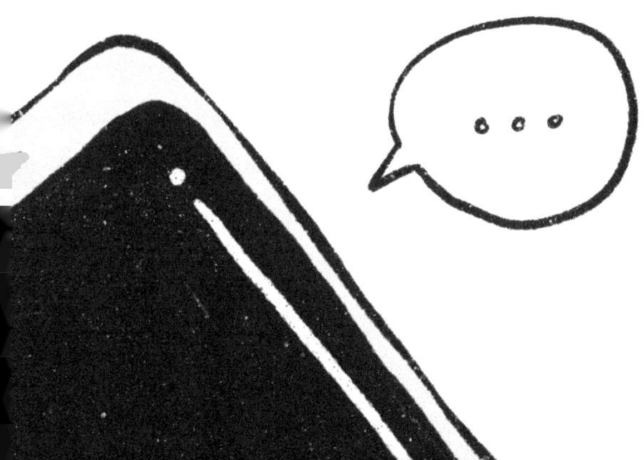

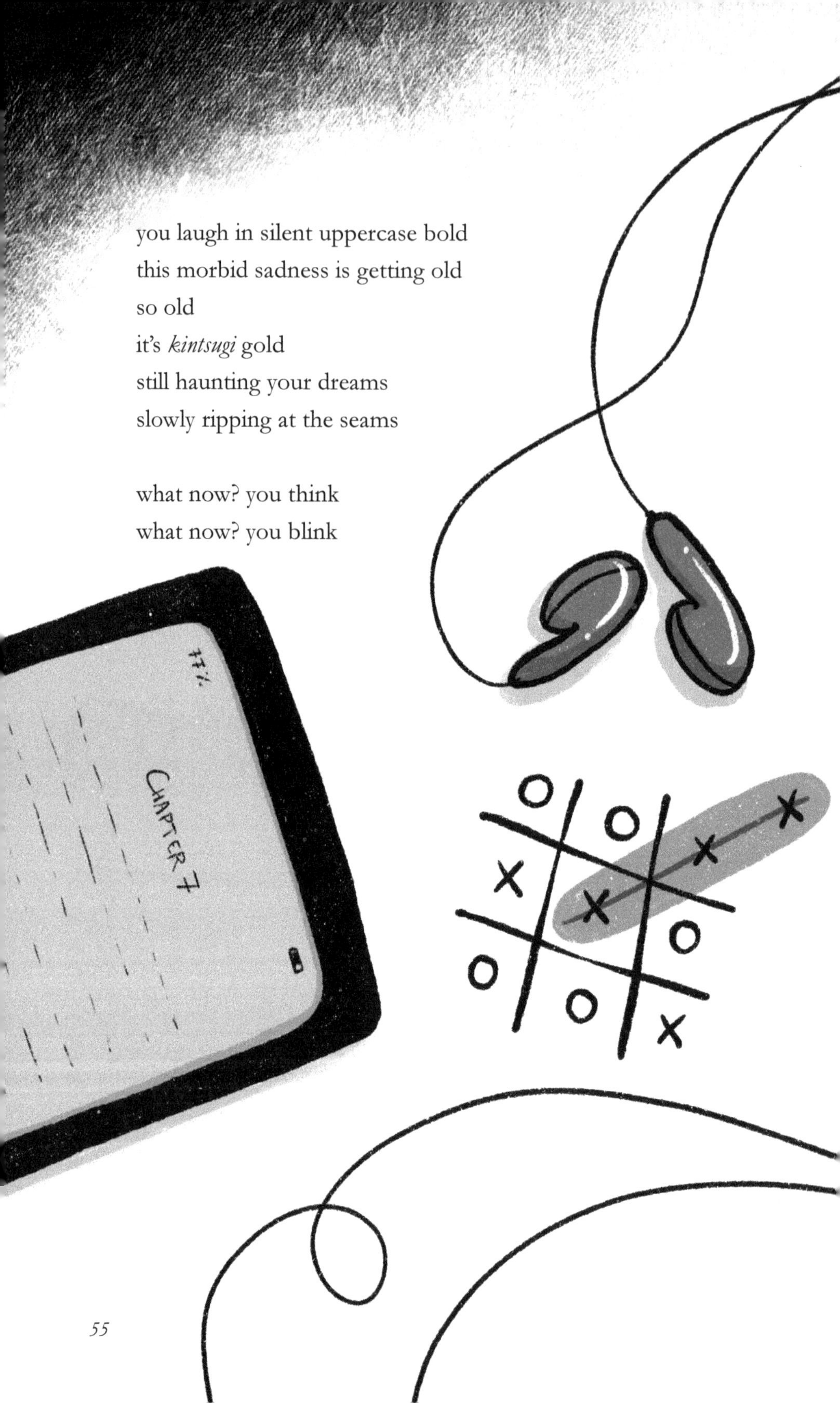

you laugh in silent uppercase bold
this morbid sadness is getting old
so old
it's *kintsugi* gold
still haunting your dreams
slowly ripping at the seams

what now? you think
what now? you blink

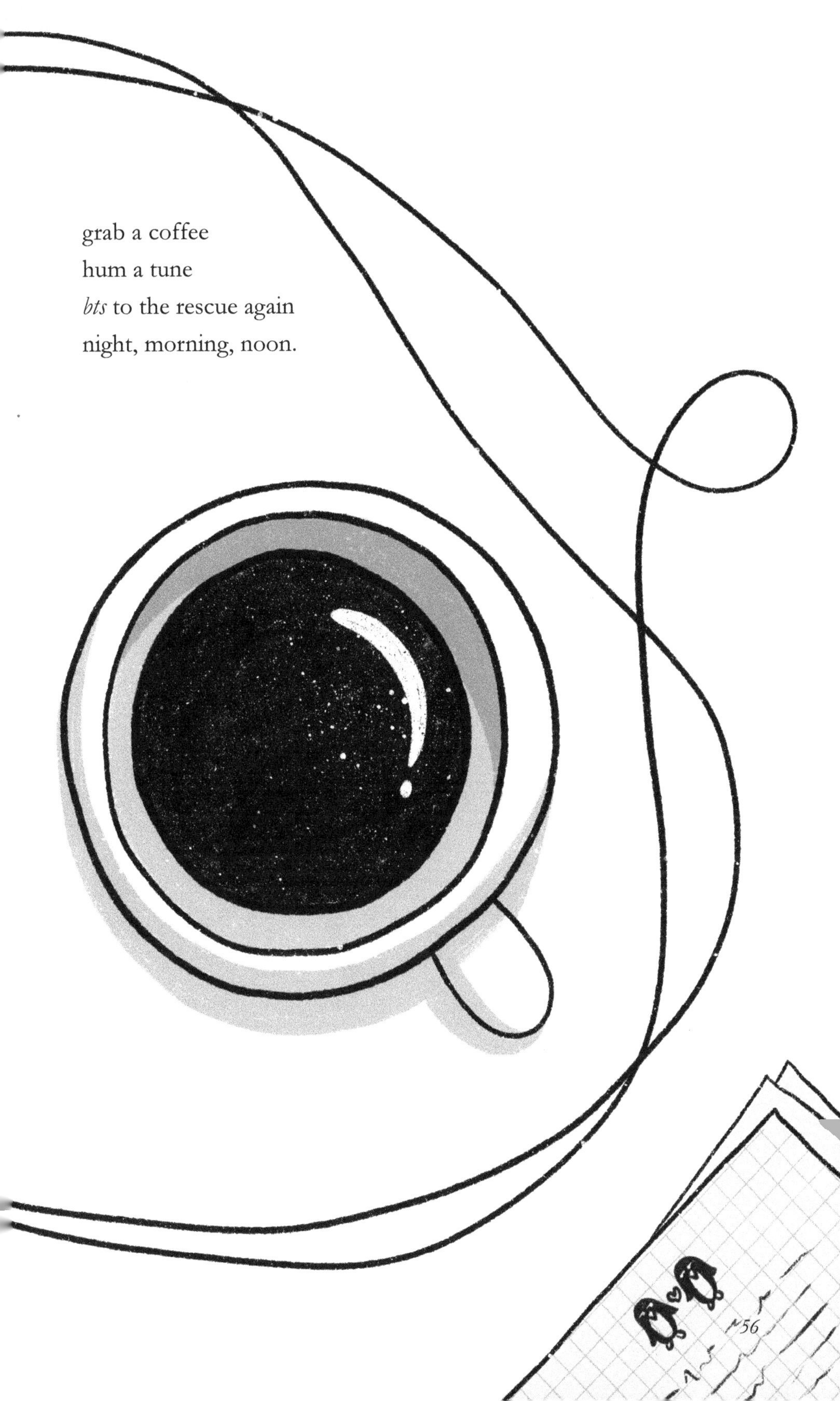

grab a coffee
hum a tune
bts to the rescue again
night, morning, noon.

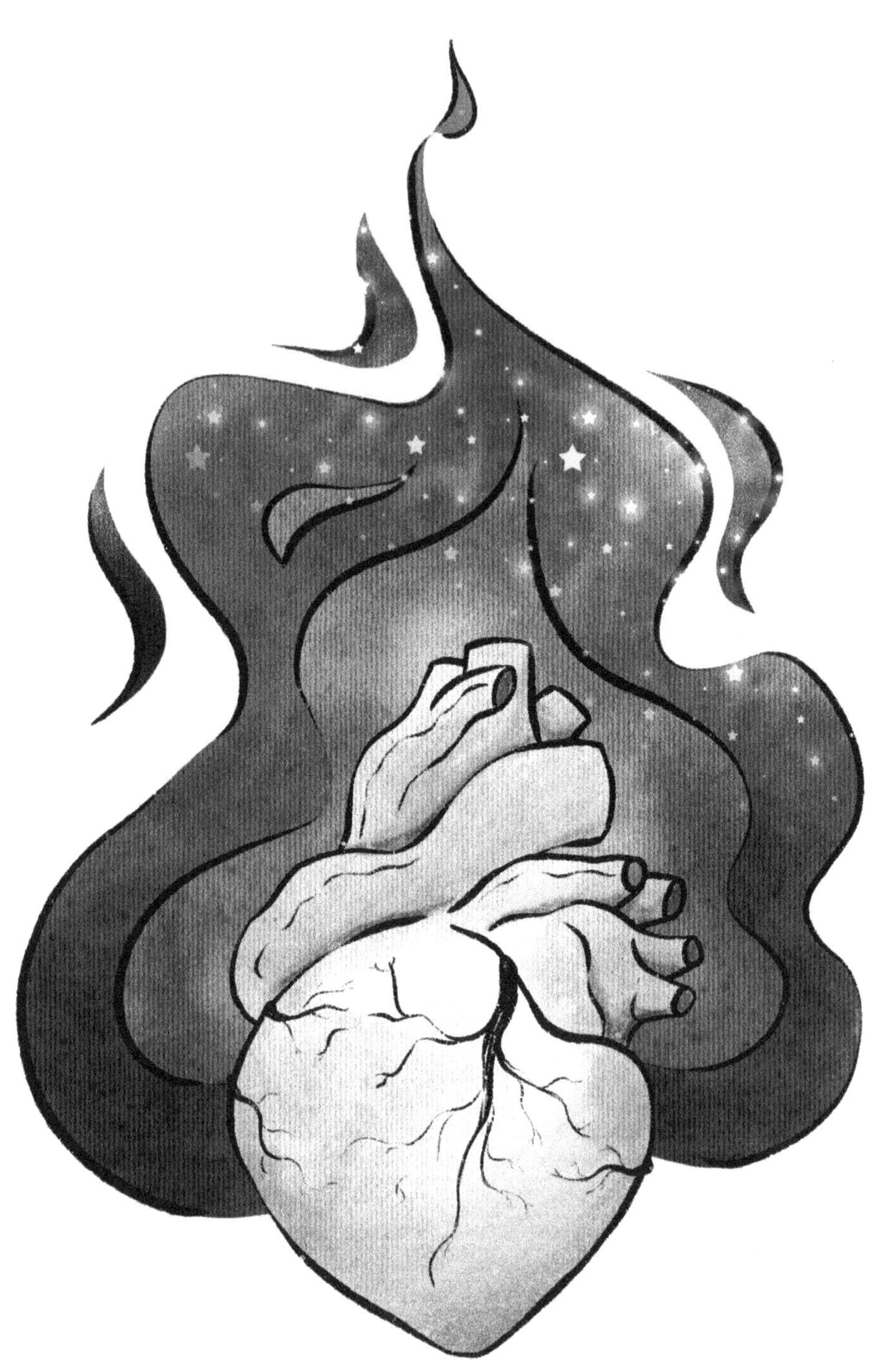

Chasm

her dislikes aren't just that
they're expressions of rage
of utmost hate

with each passing sunset and rise
she has come to realize
she cannot just like something either
she must love it with all her being
revere it with all her heart forever

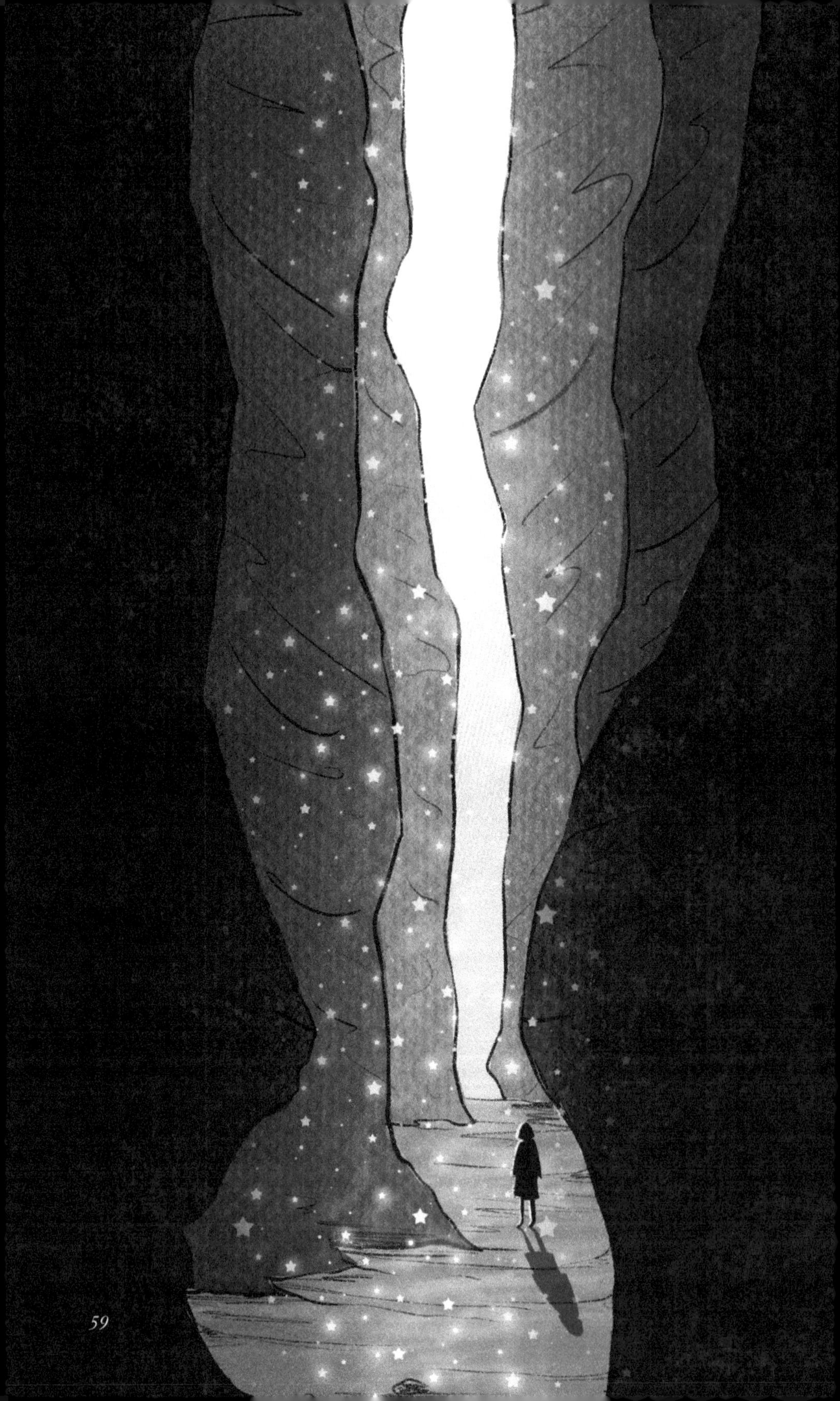

but there's a line in between those
a chasm that separates
devoted love
and burning hate

bigger than either,
deeper and wider too
is indifference, my friend
a detachment so profound, unbothered, *who?*

it's her favorite place to be, this chasm
between the swinging tides
and the two extremes
it's where her power lies
so do all her hopes, desires and dreams.

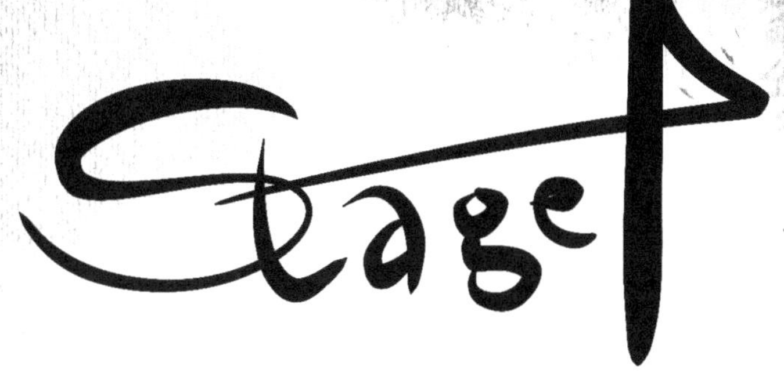

QUESTIONS

— are there even answers? —

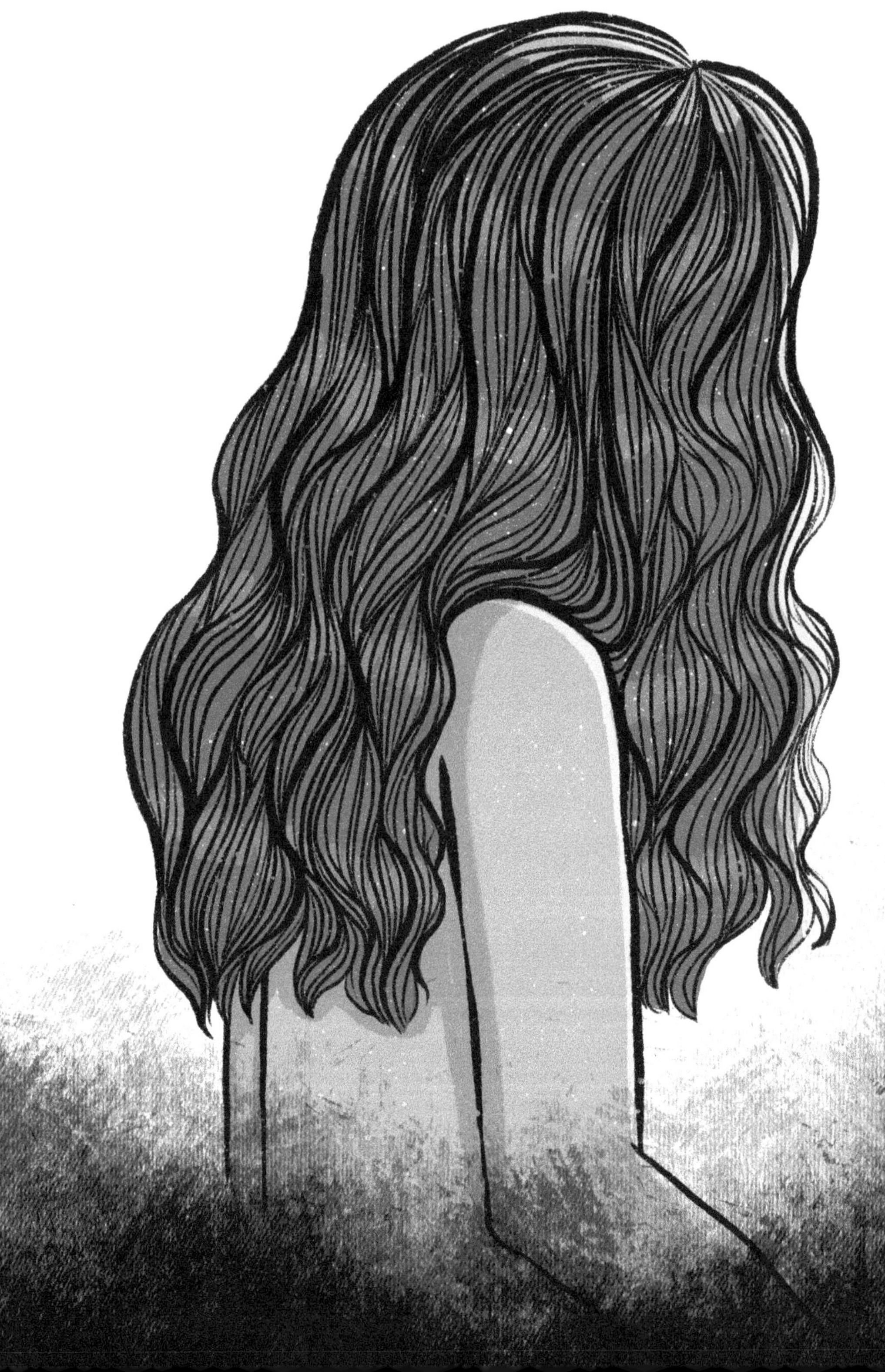

Who is she?

she's not her pain
but then…
who is she
without her pain?

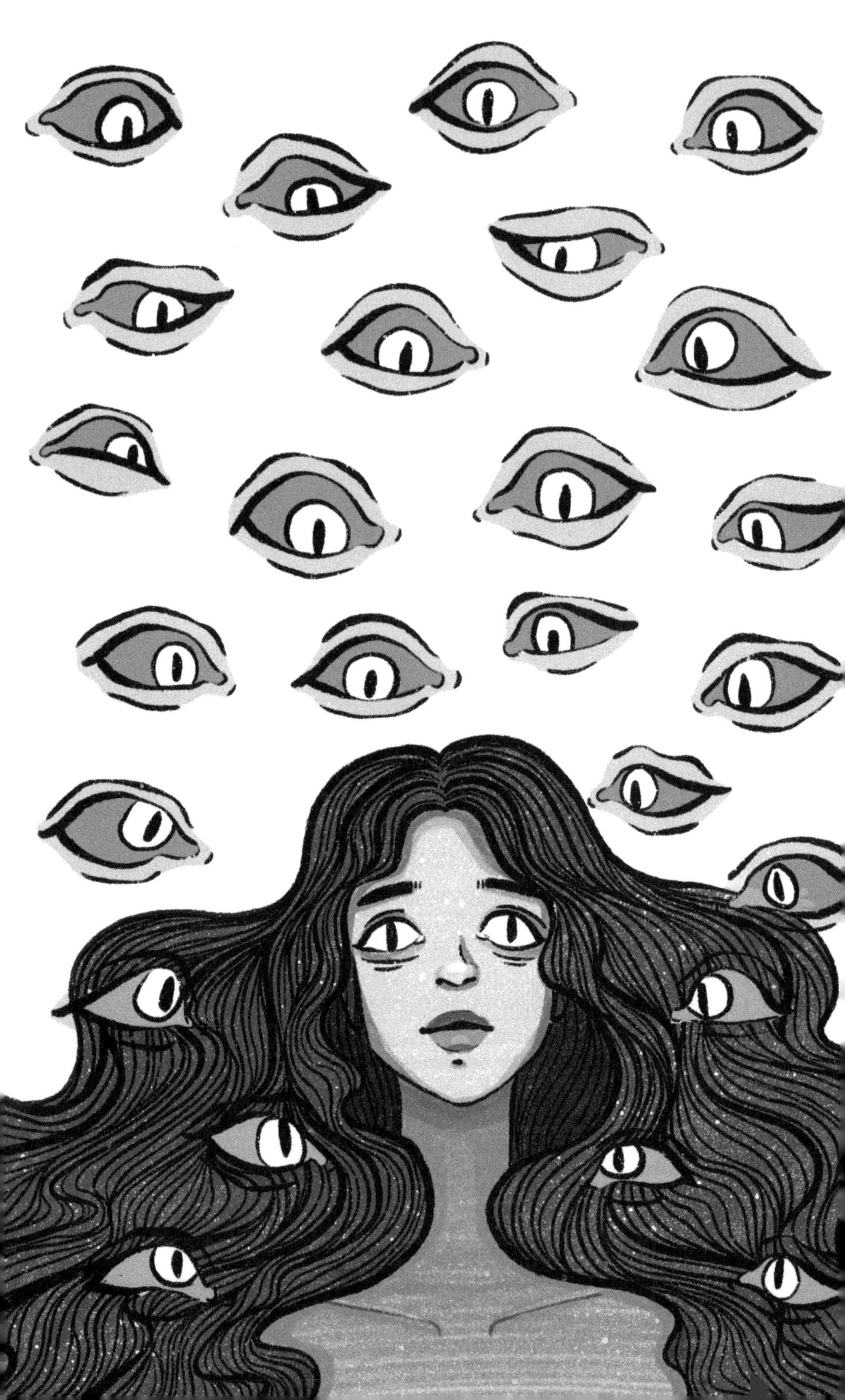

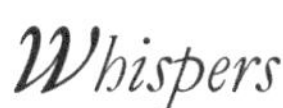

*W*hispers

whispers through the veil
i feel
little nudges, clues
something psychic
or psychosis?

whispers through the veil
i feel
like i know, but i don't
things hidden right around the bend
a different timeline, a different end

so might i dip my fingertips
in this furious, curious flow?
would it carry me through the ravines it visits
as feathery kisses, soft and slow?

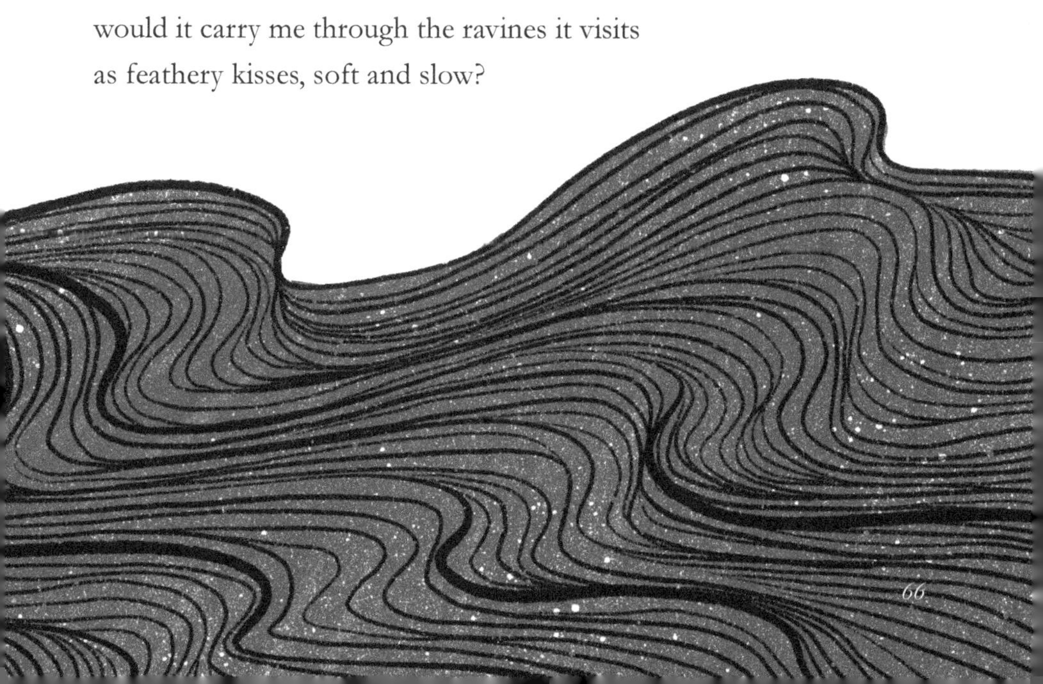

whispers through the veil
i feel

every door closed, but one
every door without, but within
but every door was the one
the one that led to you
because it all leads to you

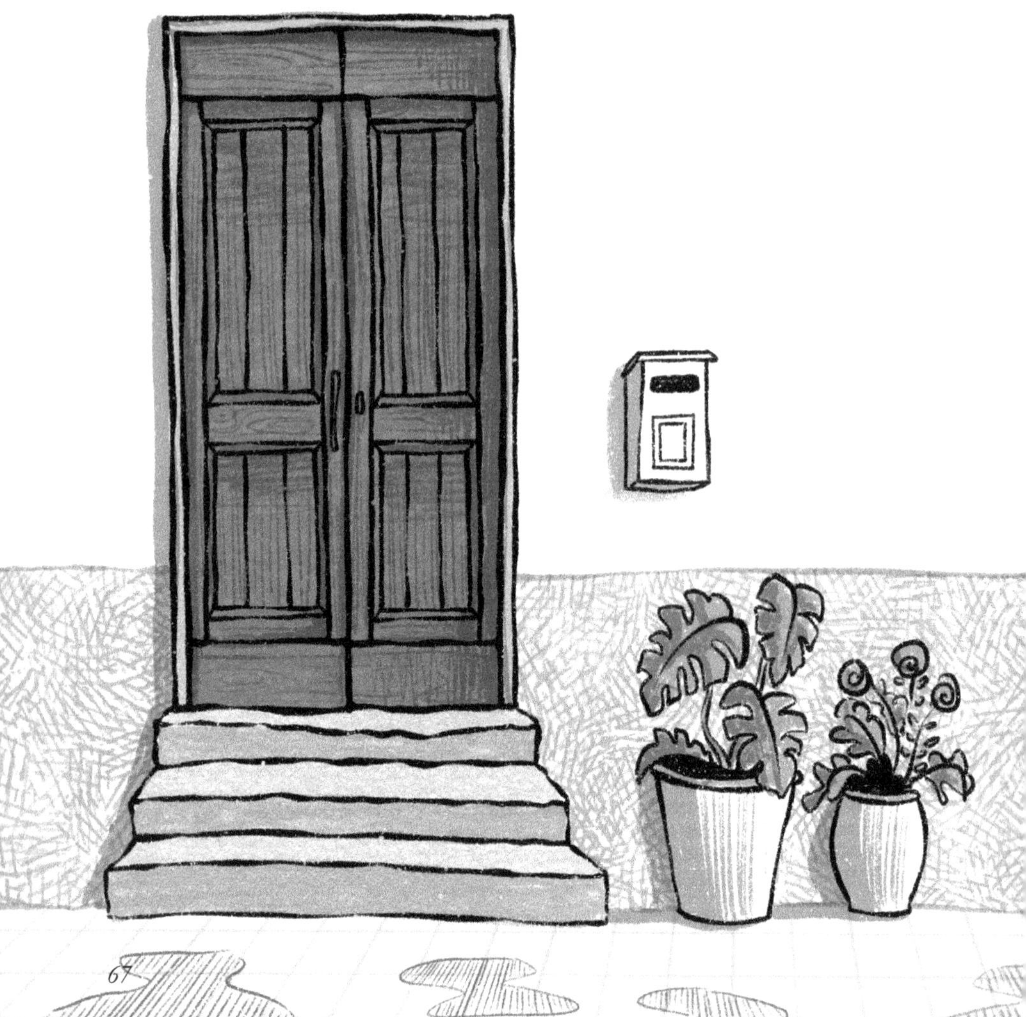

whispers through the veil
i feel
but the skeptic in me
doesn't believe still
how the pieces now click from ages ago
how they've been ushering me all along
down shrinking alleys that narrowed
till the only path remained
but all those roads were one and the same

whispers through the veil
i feel, i see
the vividest of dreams
and stuff that makes me want to scream
am i finally going crazy
or maybe just for a while
maybe i'll
tell the skeptic to lay back and smile,
and pay no heed,
as i keep listening to these
whispers through the veil.

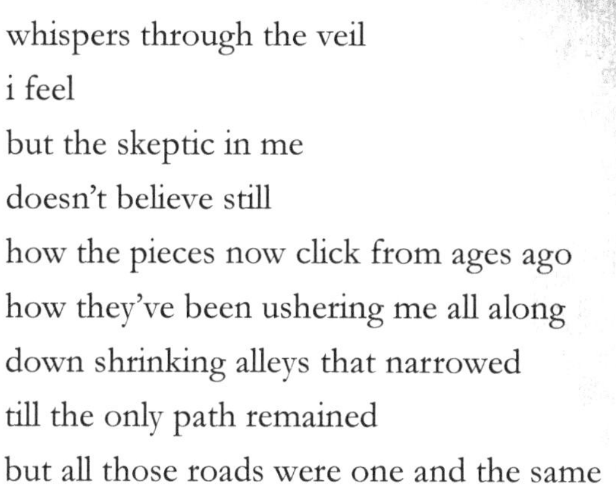

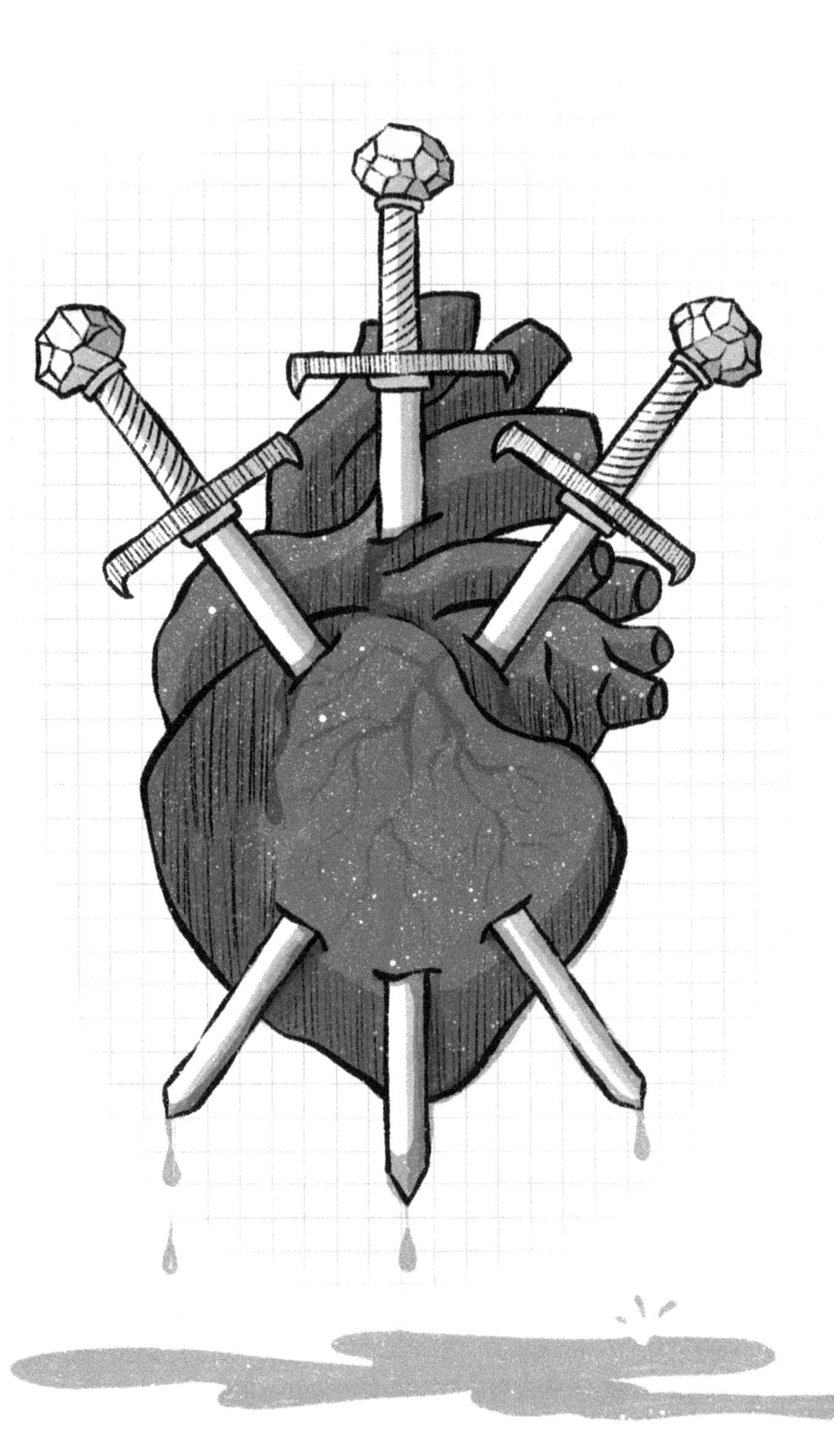

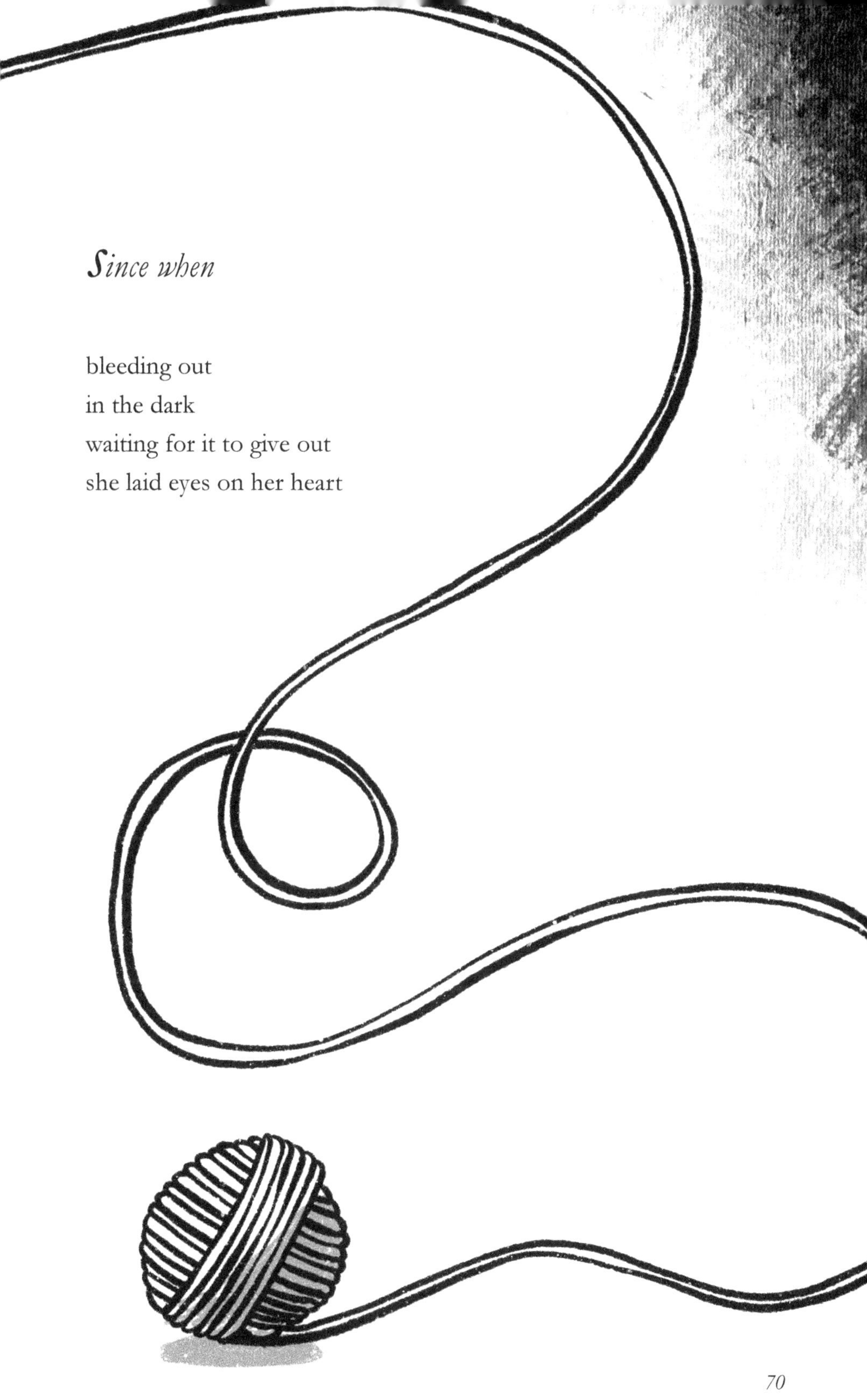

Since when

bleeding out
in the dark
waiting for it to give out
she laid eyes on her heart

barely held together at the seams,
keeping her whole,
was your name embroidered
on the walls in gold

since when was this here?
since when were you here?
since when have you been holding it up?

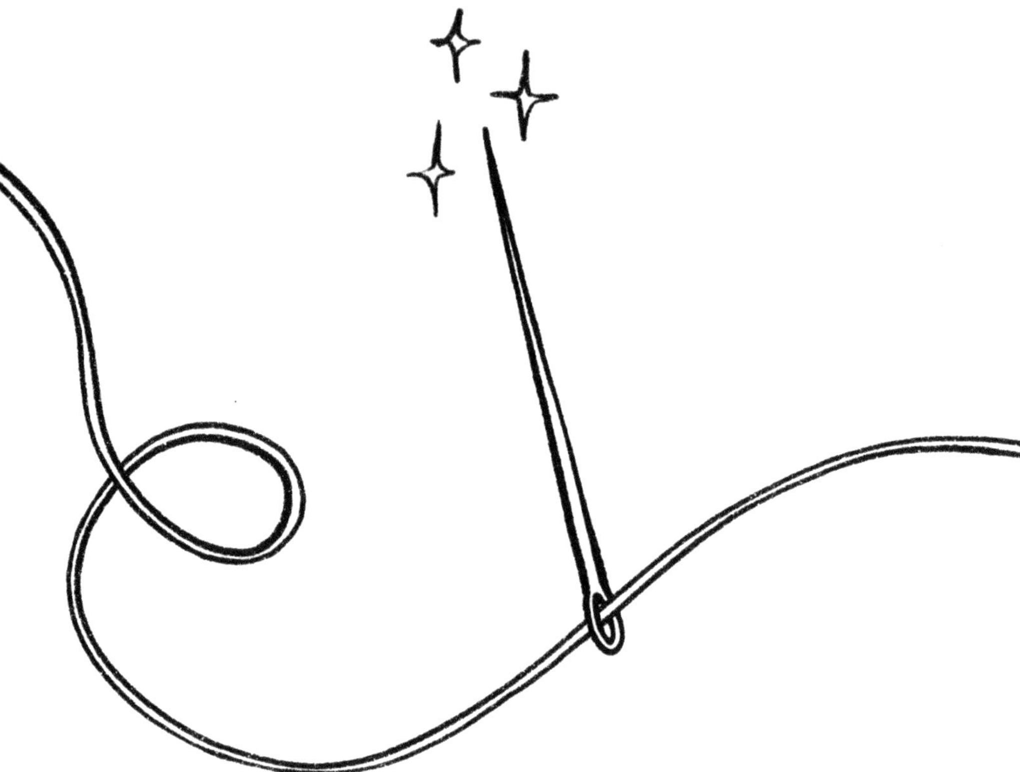

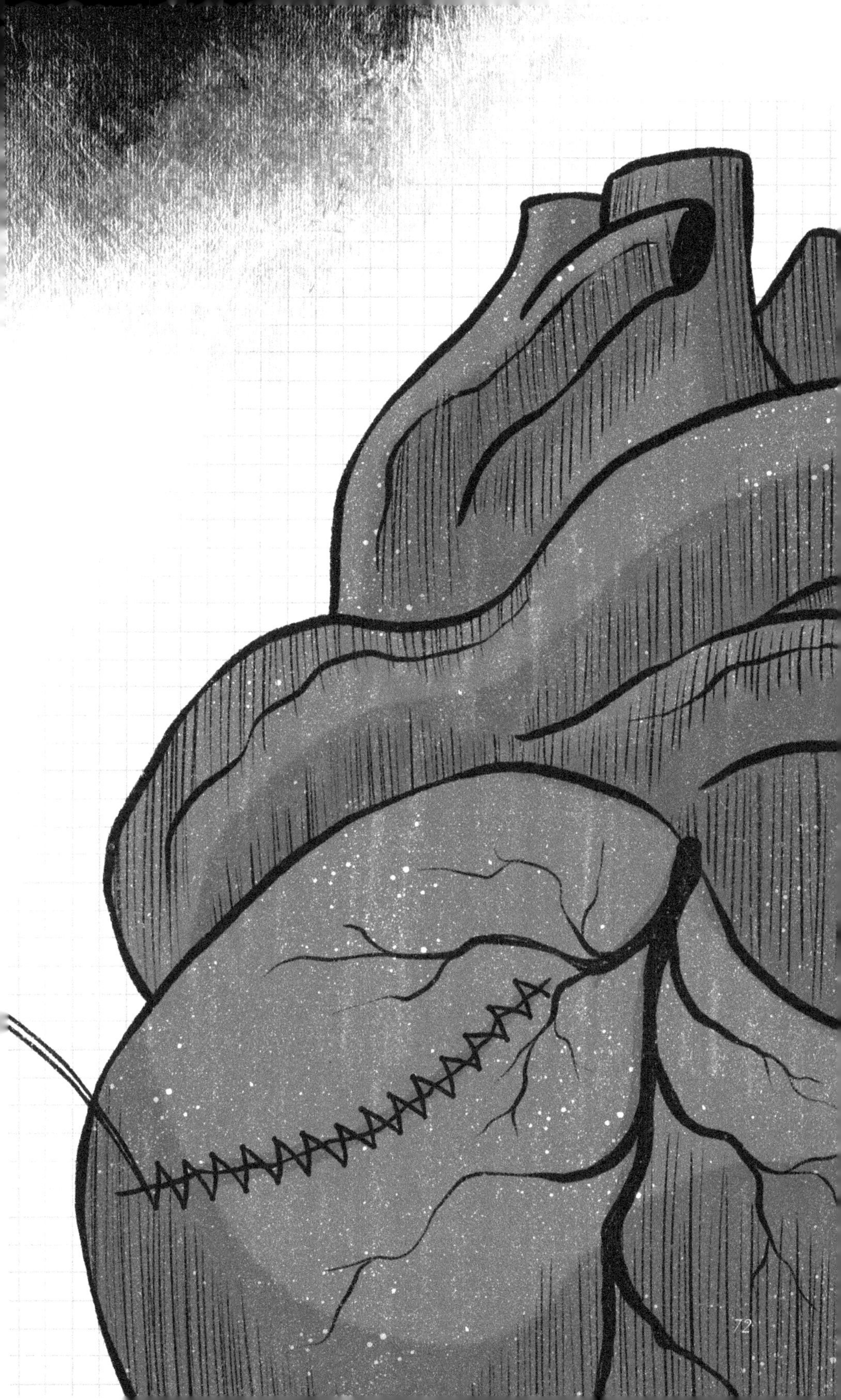

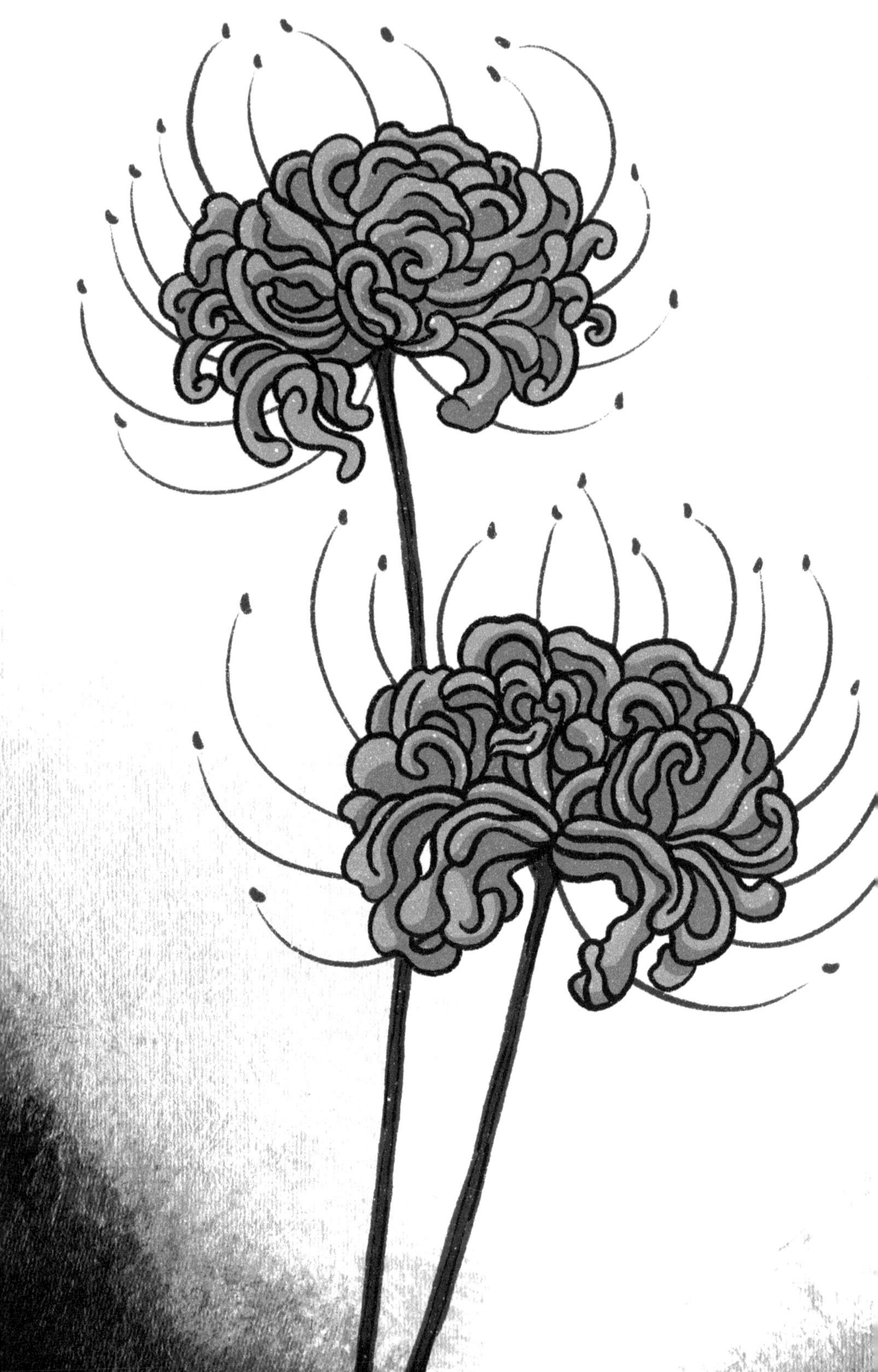

People you miss

what if it's not people from the past you miss
but people from your future?
(and you miss them terribly so)

the longing hurts
but it also heals your heart
it brims with hope
yet the sting is sharp

it's the love you feel caressing your bones
love that's forever been shining through your soul
love that's young, and love that's old
and the love that holds you soft, makes you bold

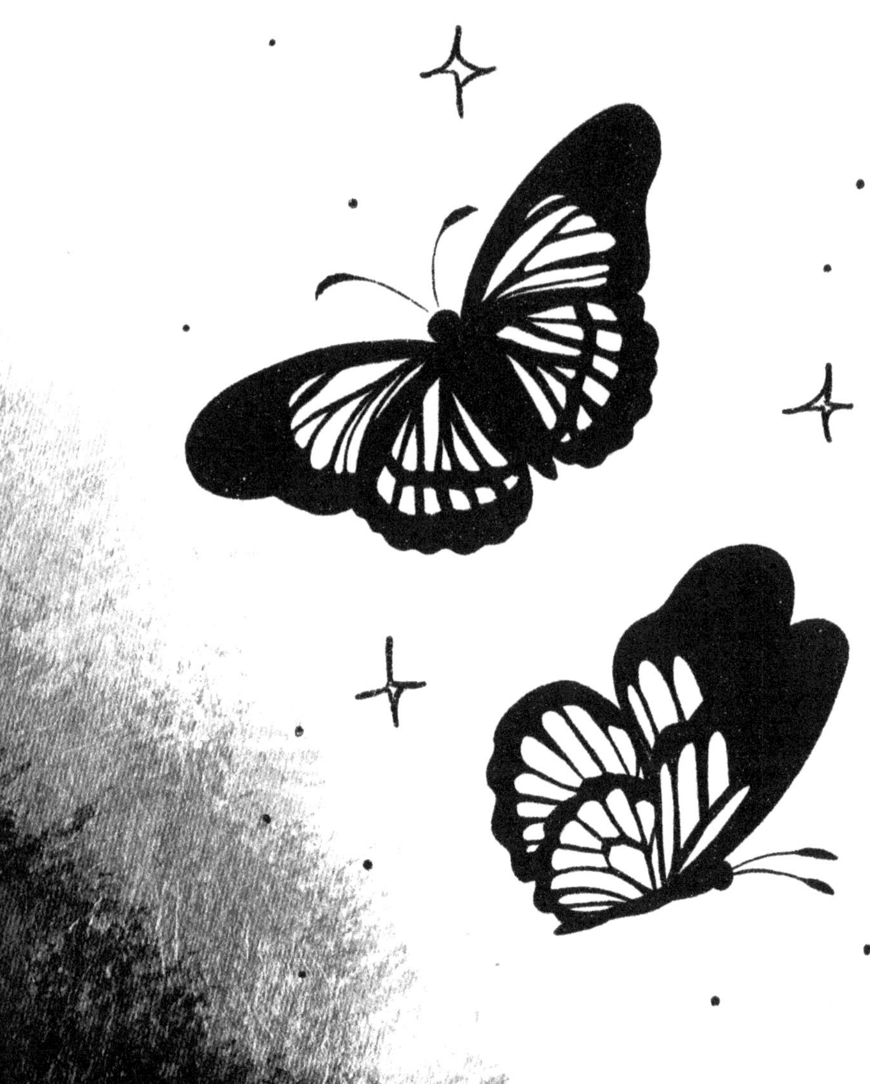

you have a knowing so deep
soon, very soon, you're going to meet

you're going to find them
or they'll find you
it doesn't matter either way
the wait doesn't matter too

because you're okay with waiting
even though you desperately wait for the wait to be over
what if it's not people from the past you miss
but people from your future?

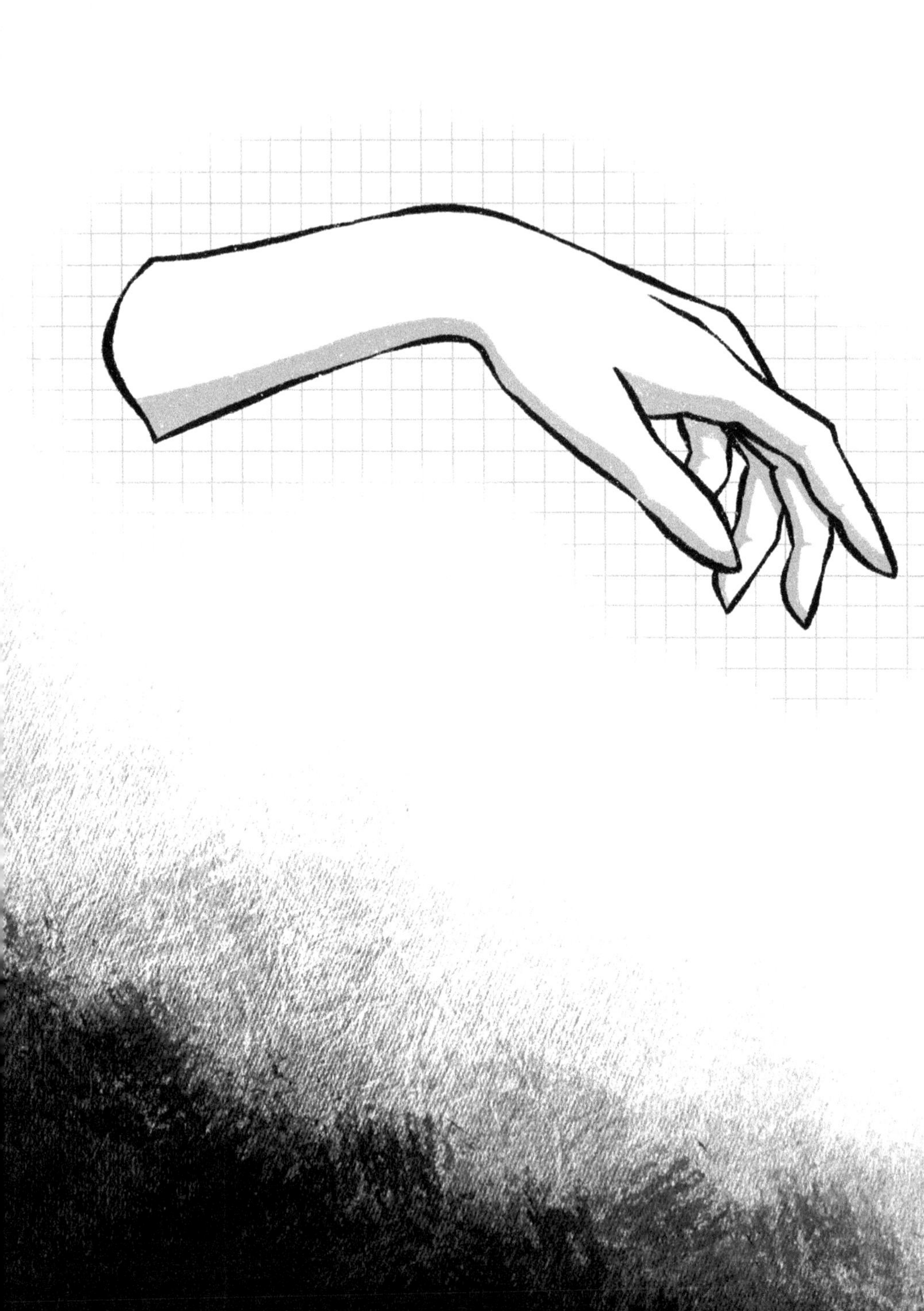

*d*ear you, dear me

dear you,
what is it like?
knowing you're safe
and that someone's got your back?
are we brave?

dear you,
i know, there are good people
with love, tender and true
i haven't met them yet
have you?

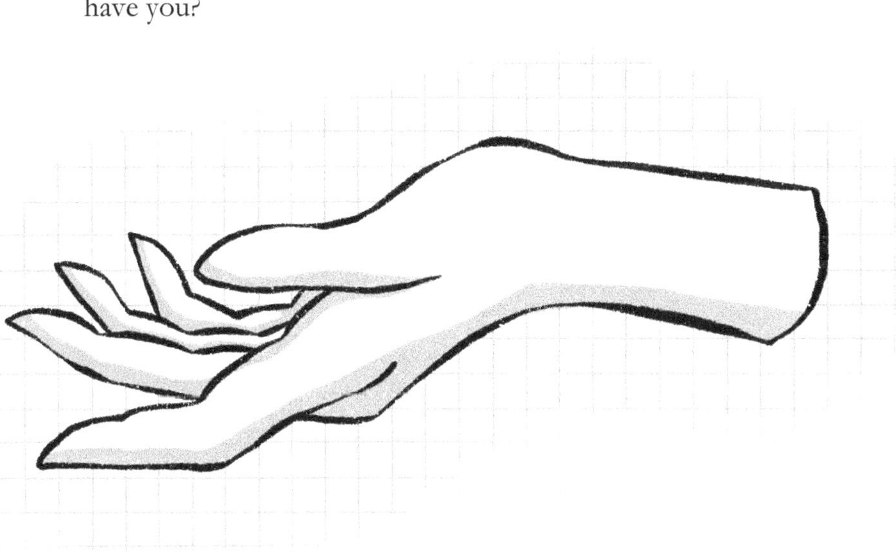

dear you,
it hurts right now
i can't remember when it didn't
does it get better?
won't you give me a hint?

dear you,
are we still waiting?
procrastinating?
"tomorrow. do it tomorrow.
let's just live one more day."
are you still lying to yourself this way?

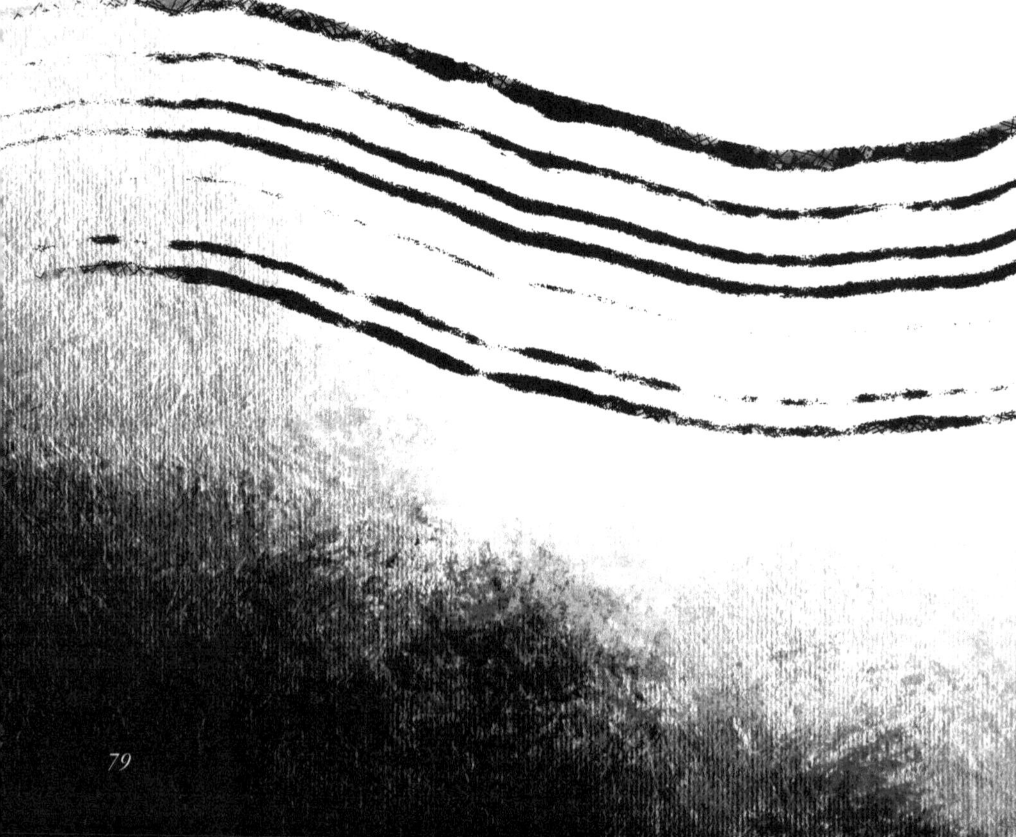

dear you,
dear me,
are we there yet?
are we free?

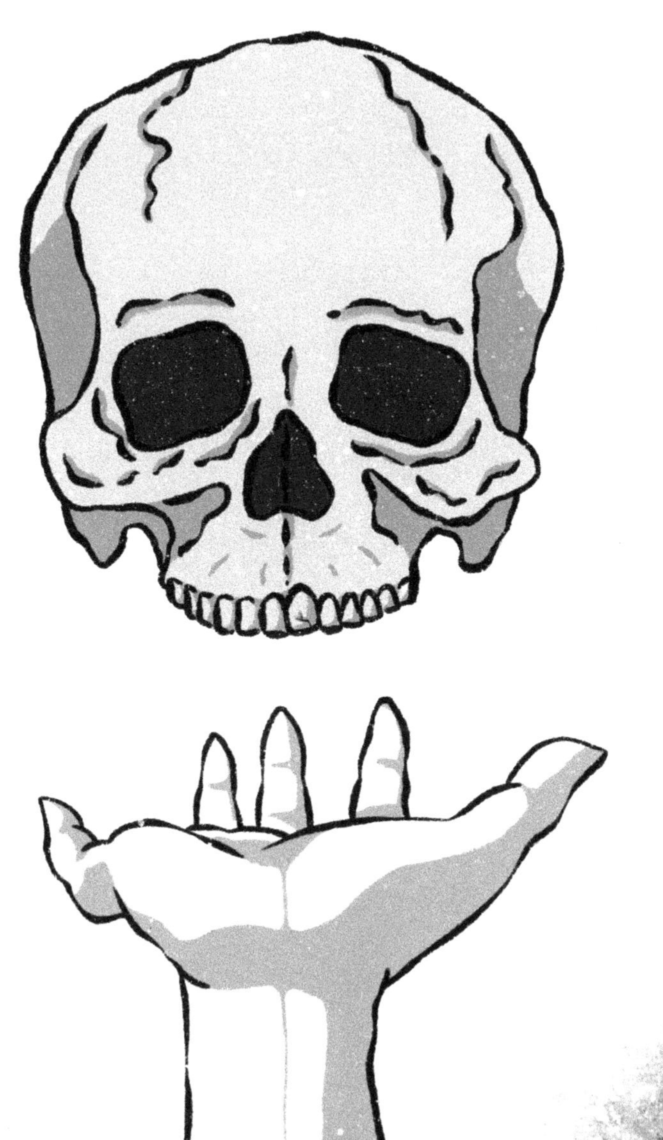

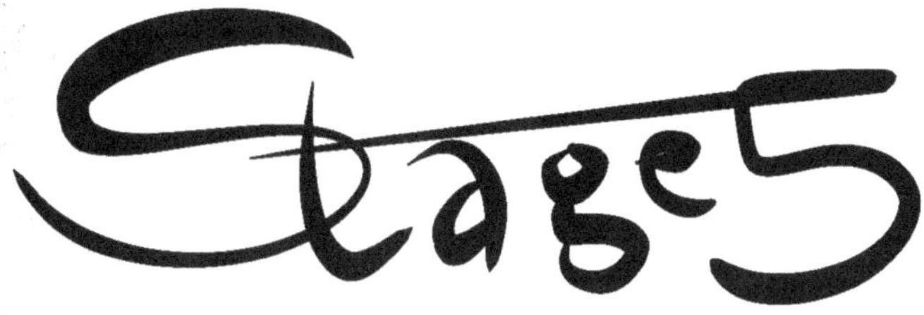

LOVE

— *she meets herself* —

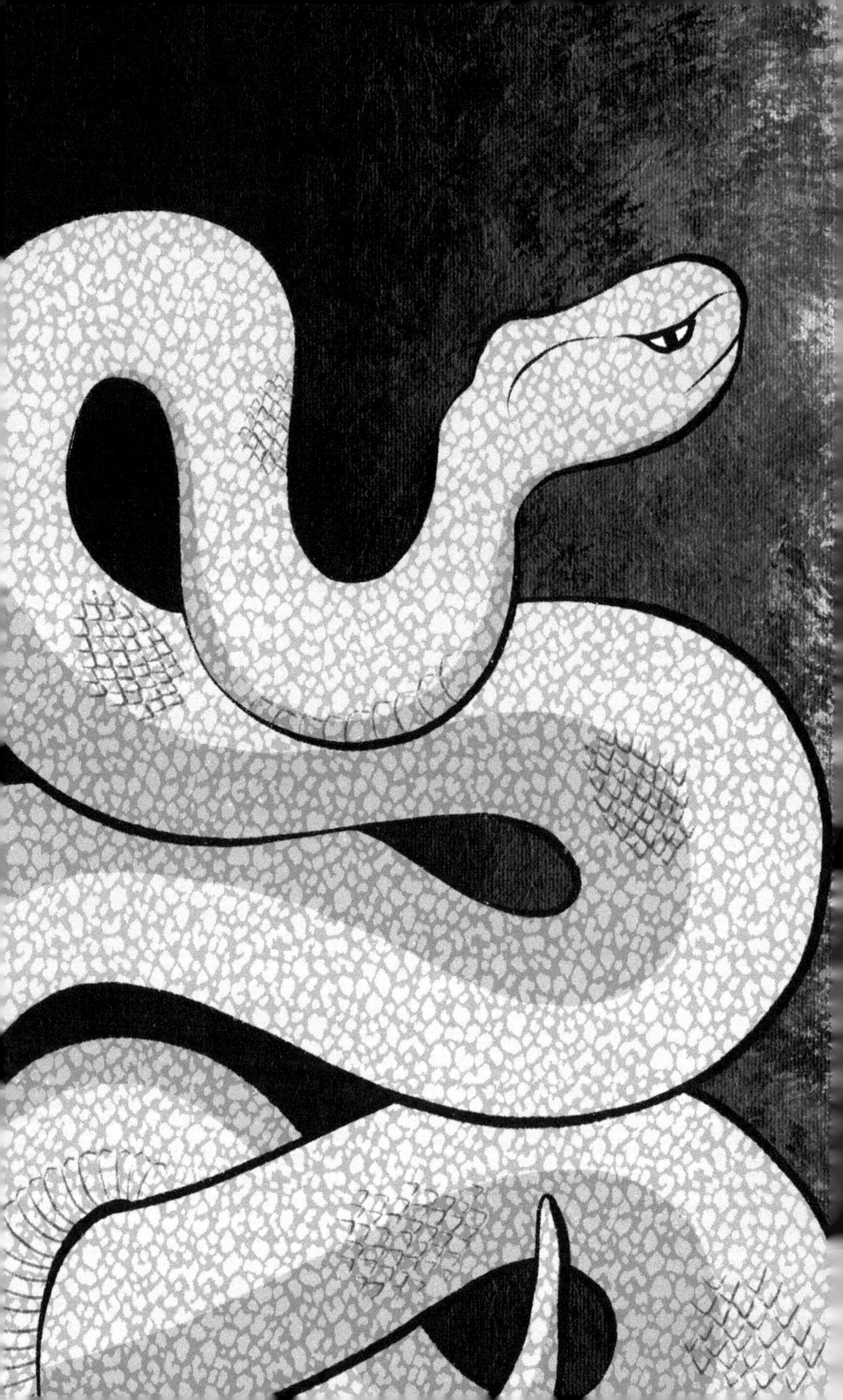

Now that you've met you

you let the trash take itself out
now watch the magic unfold
you've been walking in their shoes for too long
obeying, doing as you're told

it's time to step into your own
and set it all down
everything that was never yours to carry
drop it, let them drown

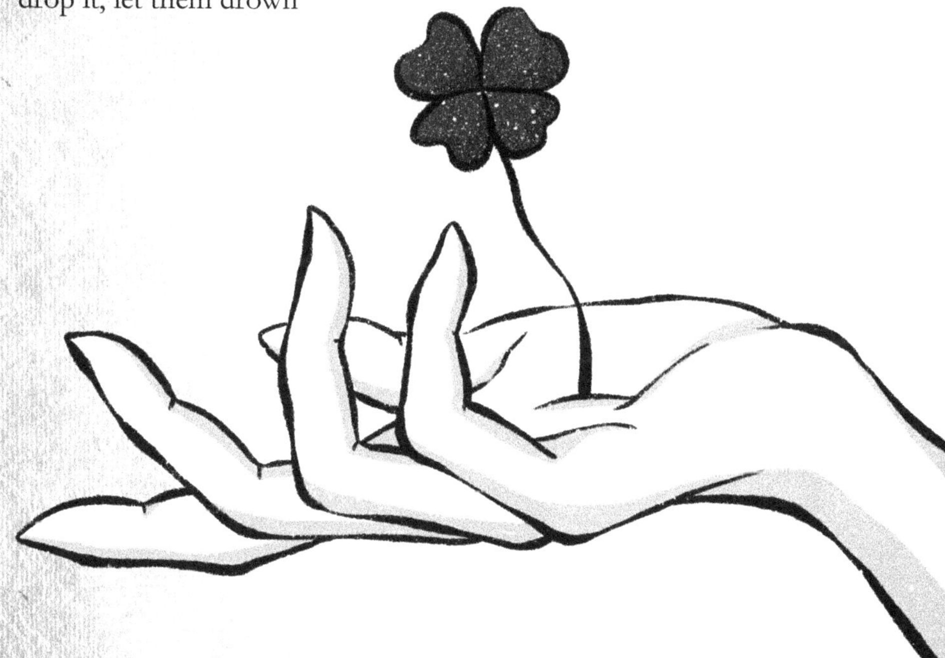

how does it feel
to finally breathe, to float
when you're no longer afraid
to ~~rock~~ wreck the bloody boat

the permission was never theirs to give
to allow your love for you
it's not important, it never was
it has always been up to you

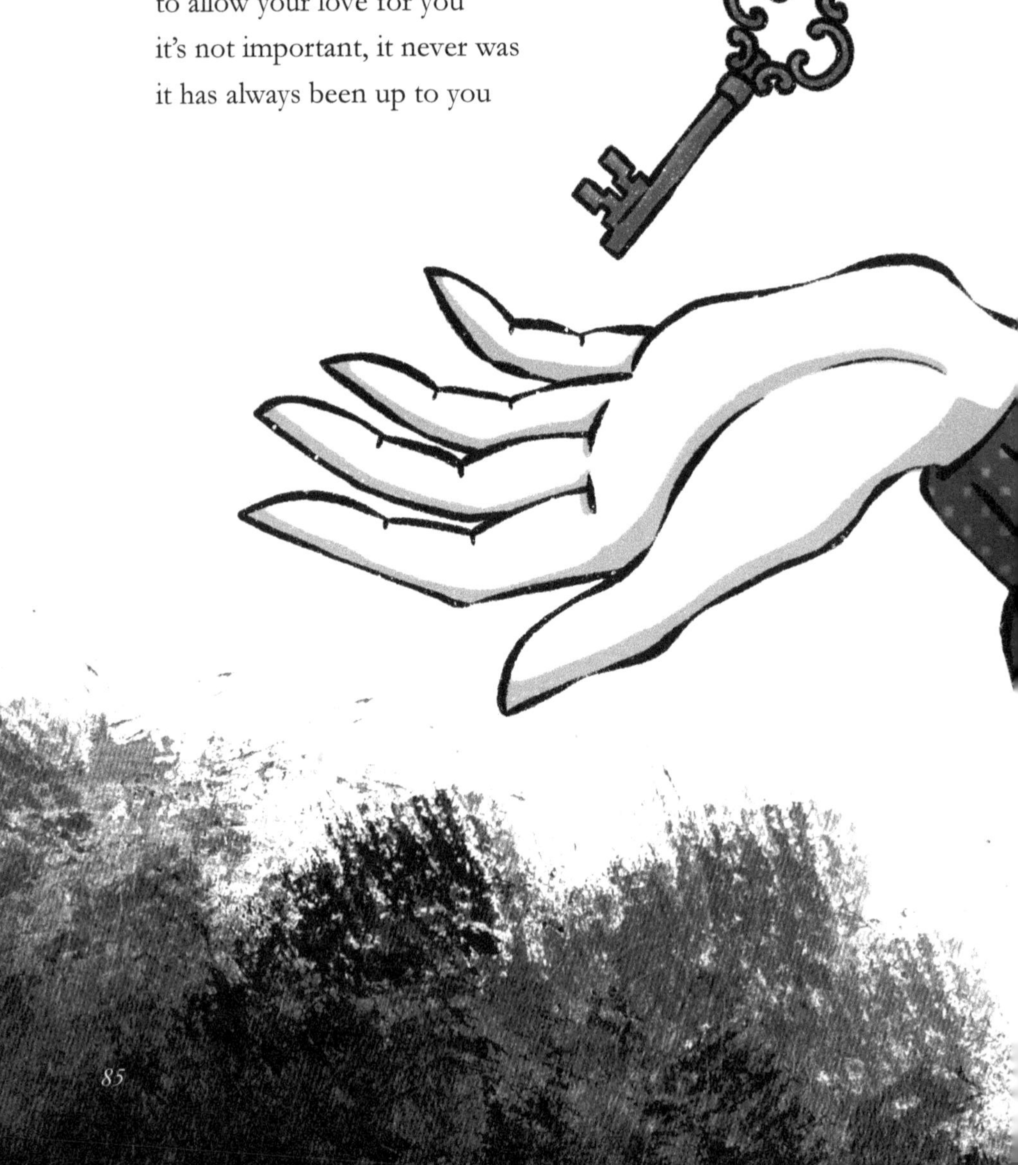

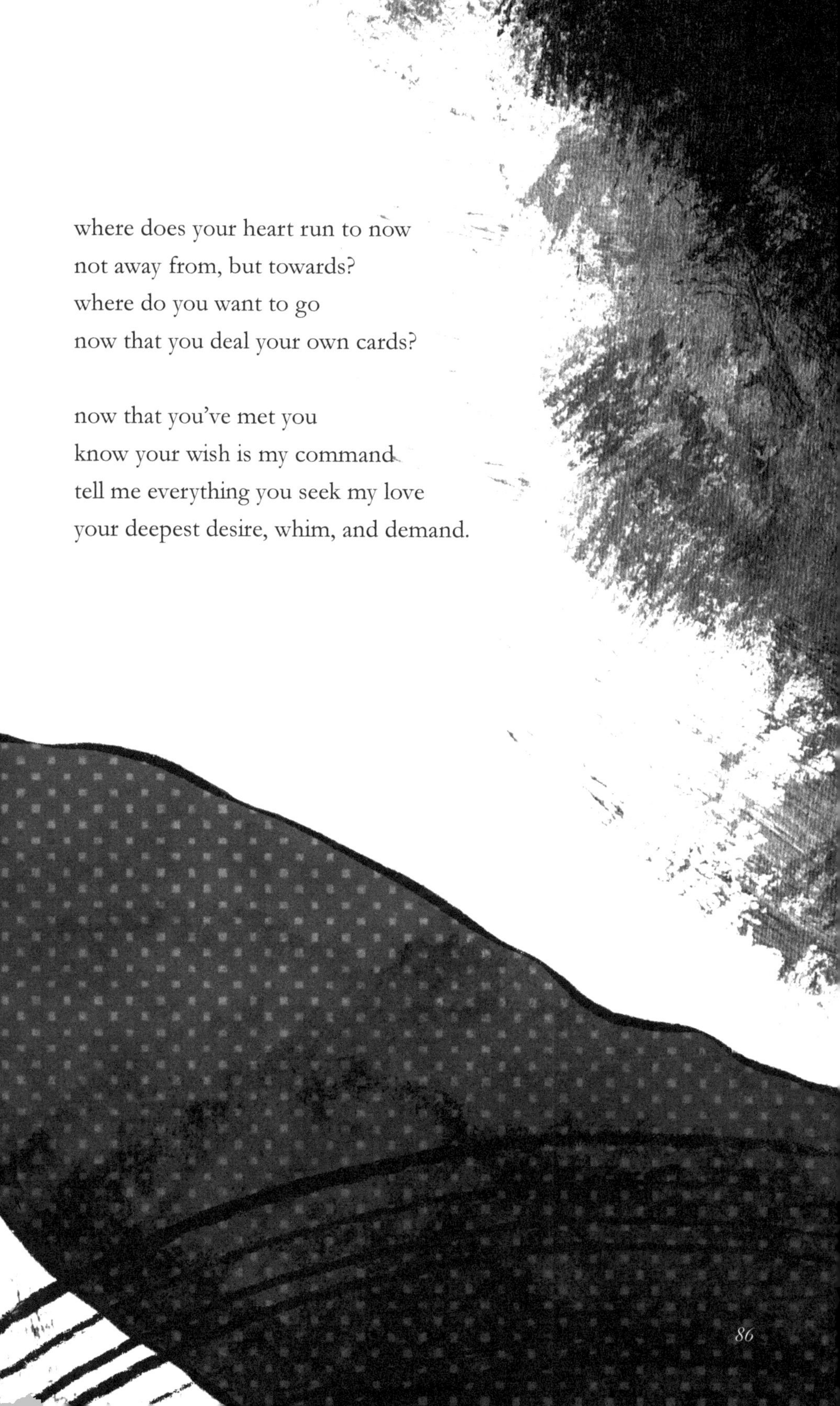

where does your heart run to now
not away from, but towards?
where do you want to go
now that you deal your own cards?

now that you've met you
know your wish is my command
tell me everything you seek my love
your deepest desire, whim, and demand.

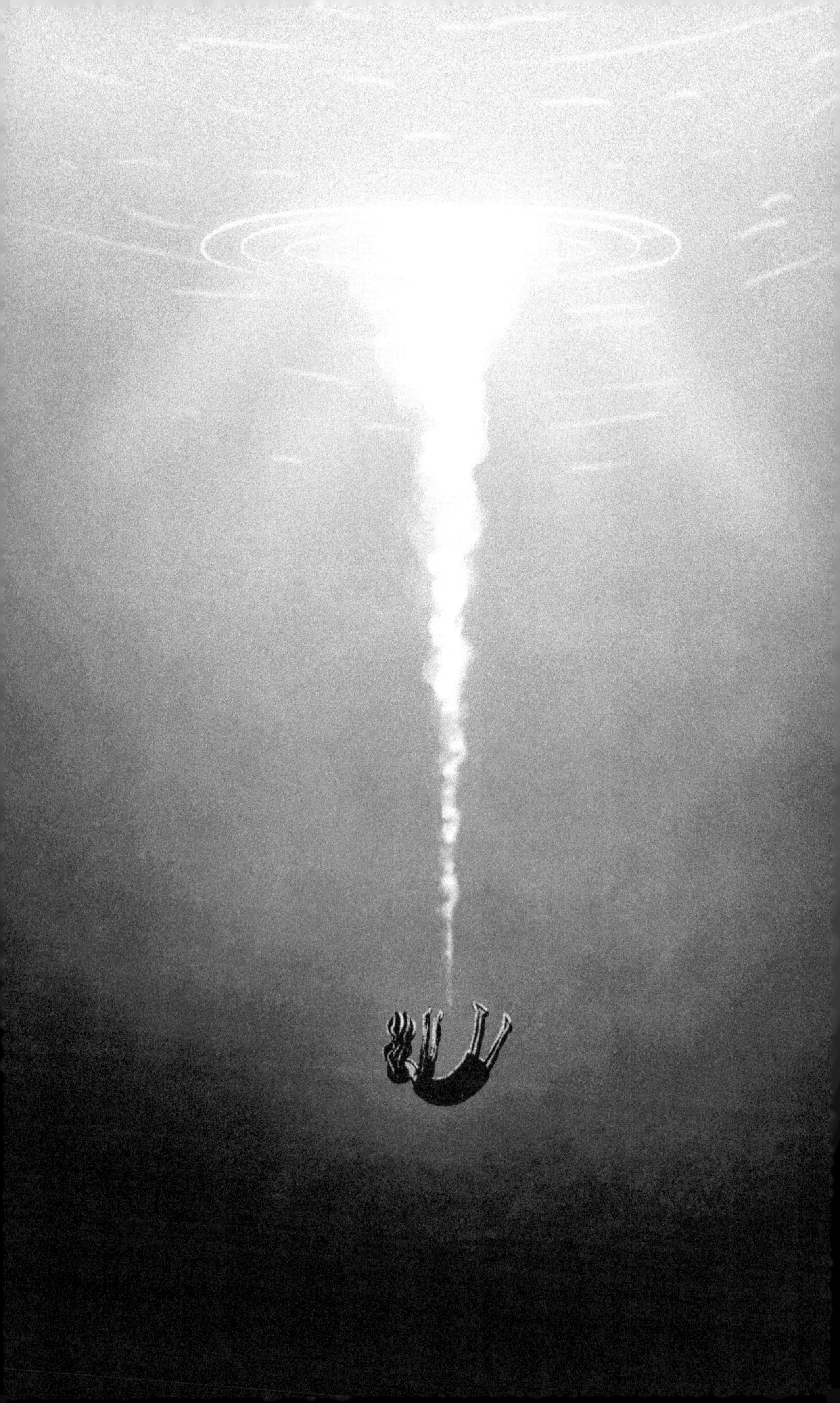

depths

who hurt you, baby girl?
who gave you all this pain
made you go so deep
into depths no light has lain
your sleepless nights
being never what they seem
mornings repeating
every terror-soaked dream

who hurt you, my love?
pushed you down so deep
to depths that made you break
depths that made you seek
and depths that made you find me
depths that made me find you
because i was there too

i didn't know you'd catch me here
in crevices, dark and cold
where love doesn't exist
yet it's been here all along
i've been here
and you've been here
and i see you now
i see you shine
do you see me yet?
is it time?

the depths aren't scary anymore
it's warm too, it's home
it's soft, and it sizzles
melting skin, bone, the old
it's sharp too
it's heavy
it's the lightest i've been
i'm bubbling gold, *kintsugi*

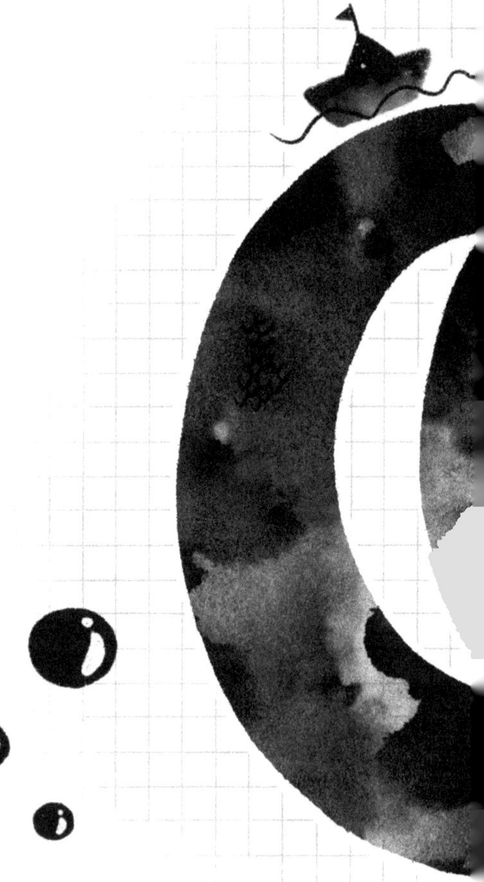

my love, these depths are yours, as am i
raw power, dark divine
it's okay now
these depths are perfectly fine
these depths that made you shine
these depths that made you mine.

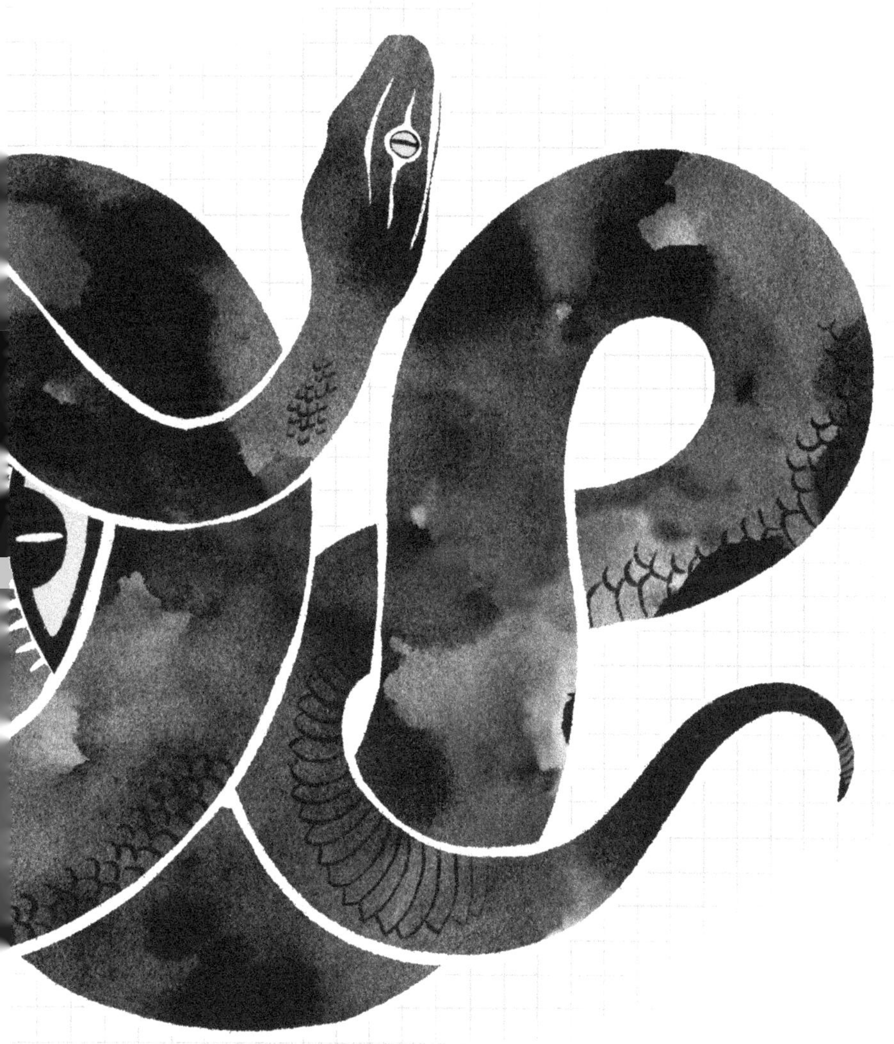

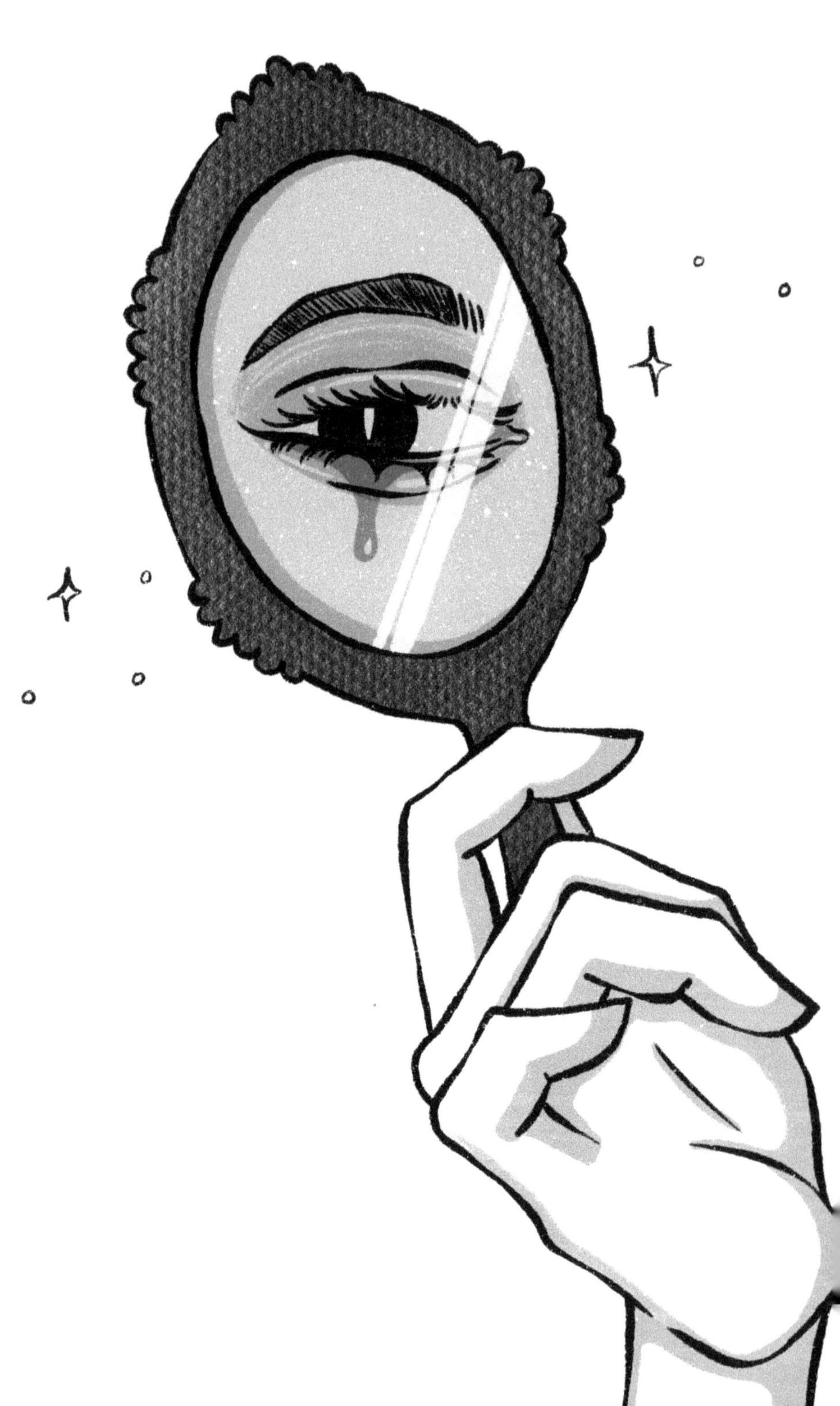

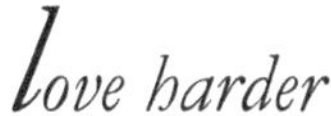

love harder

it's on days like these
nights like these
you need to love yourself harder

when you can't find anything in you to love
you must love yourself harder

when you feel repulsive,
like you're the monster
love yourself harder

when you feel like you can't
and the hate gets too strong
you love yourself harder

on days like these
and nights like these
when you want to end it all
and sabotage is all you see
you need to love yourself just a little more
and a bit more still

breathe, you've got you
even if it's the only thing you do,
again, and again, and once more, and twice more,
go on and love yourself harder.

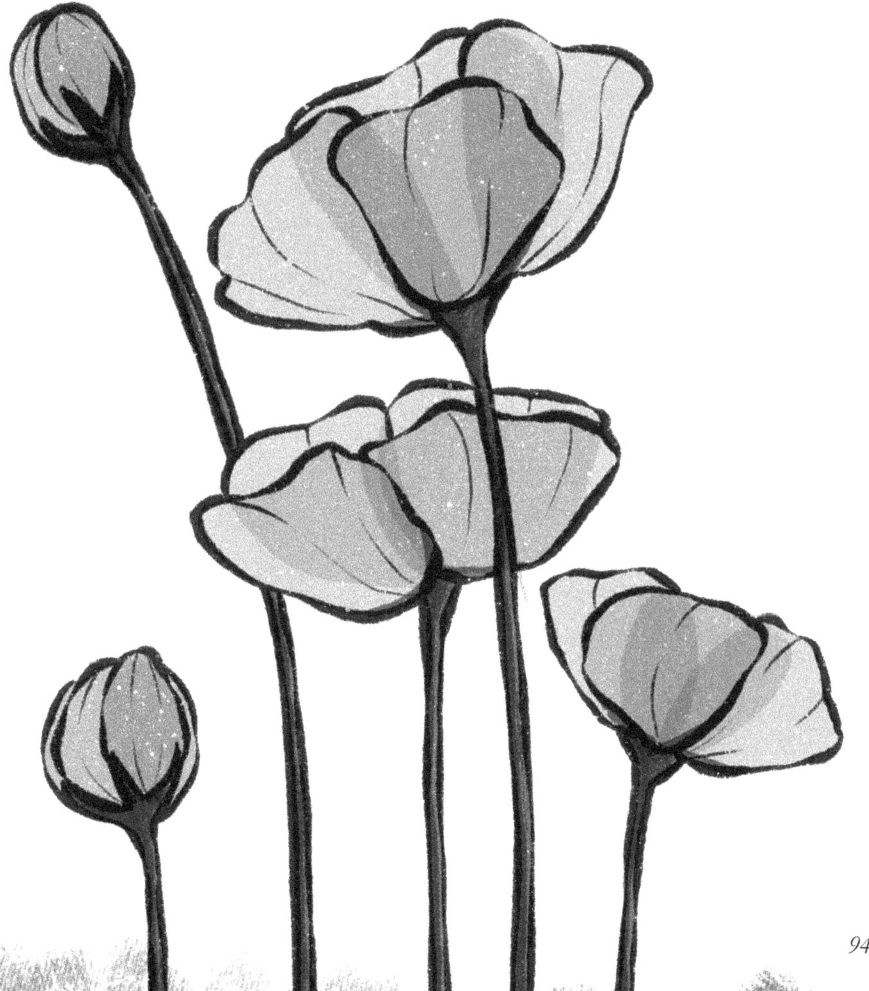

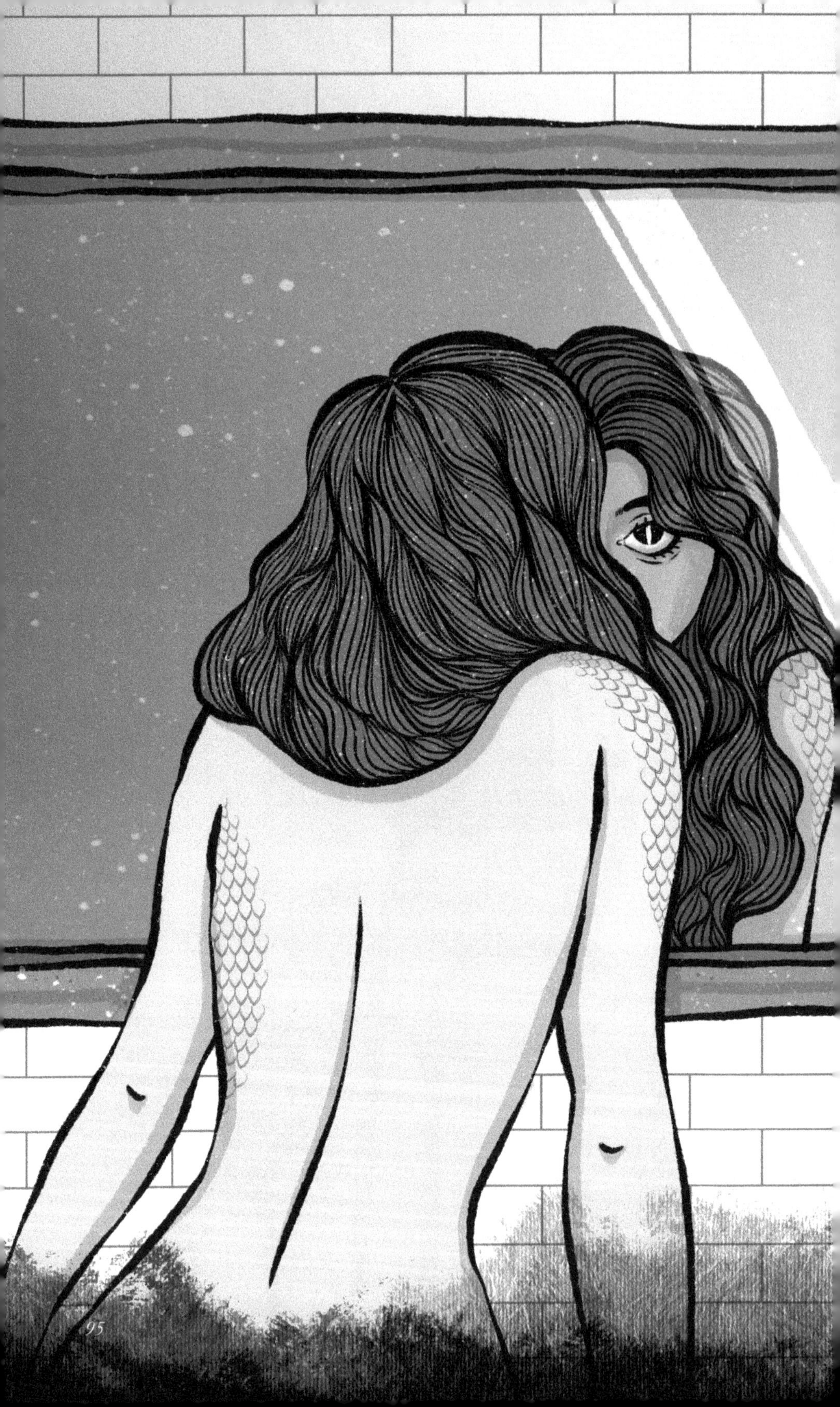

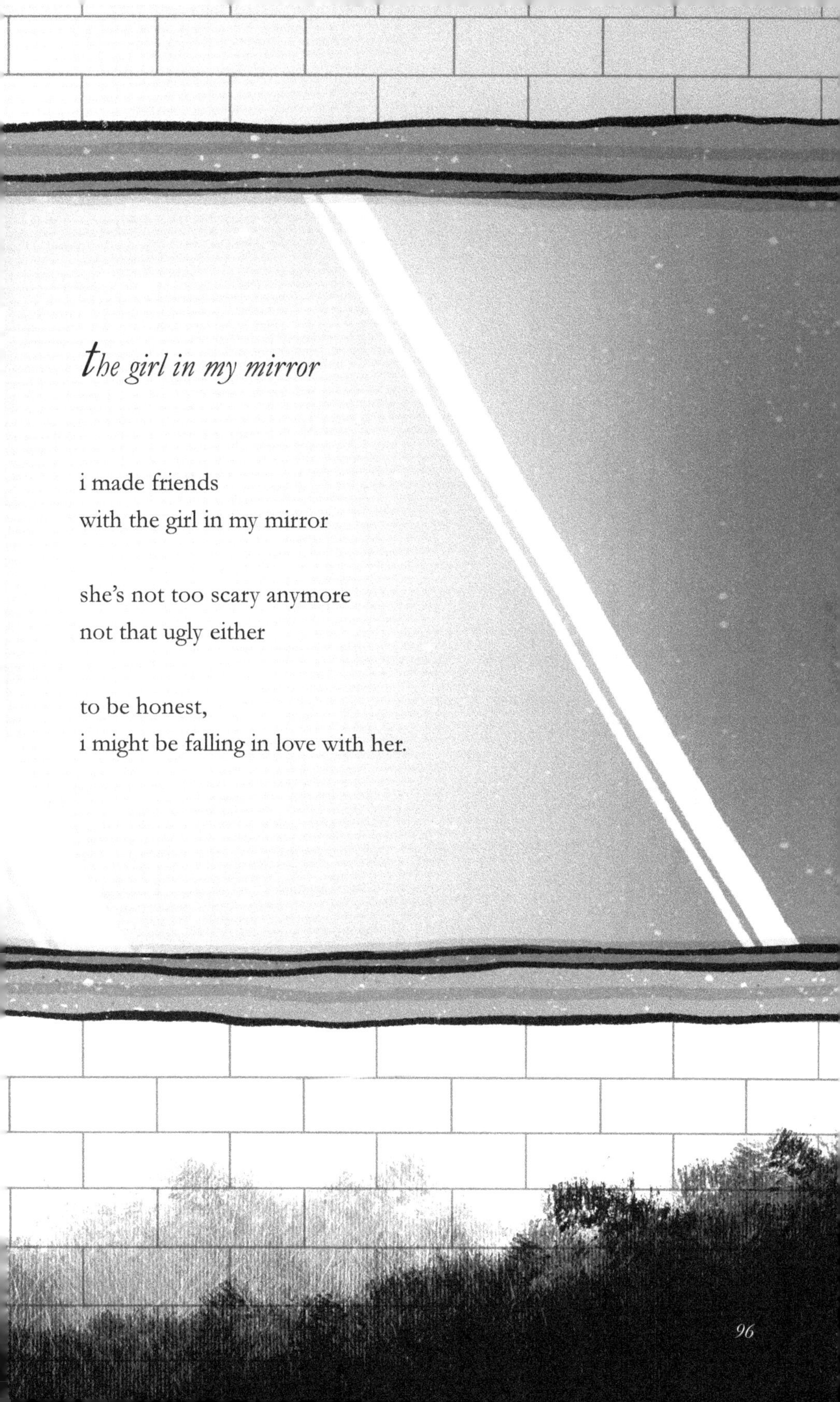

*t*he girl in my mirror

i made friends
with the girl in my mirror

she's not too scary anymore
not that ugly either

to be honest,
i might be falling in love with her.

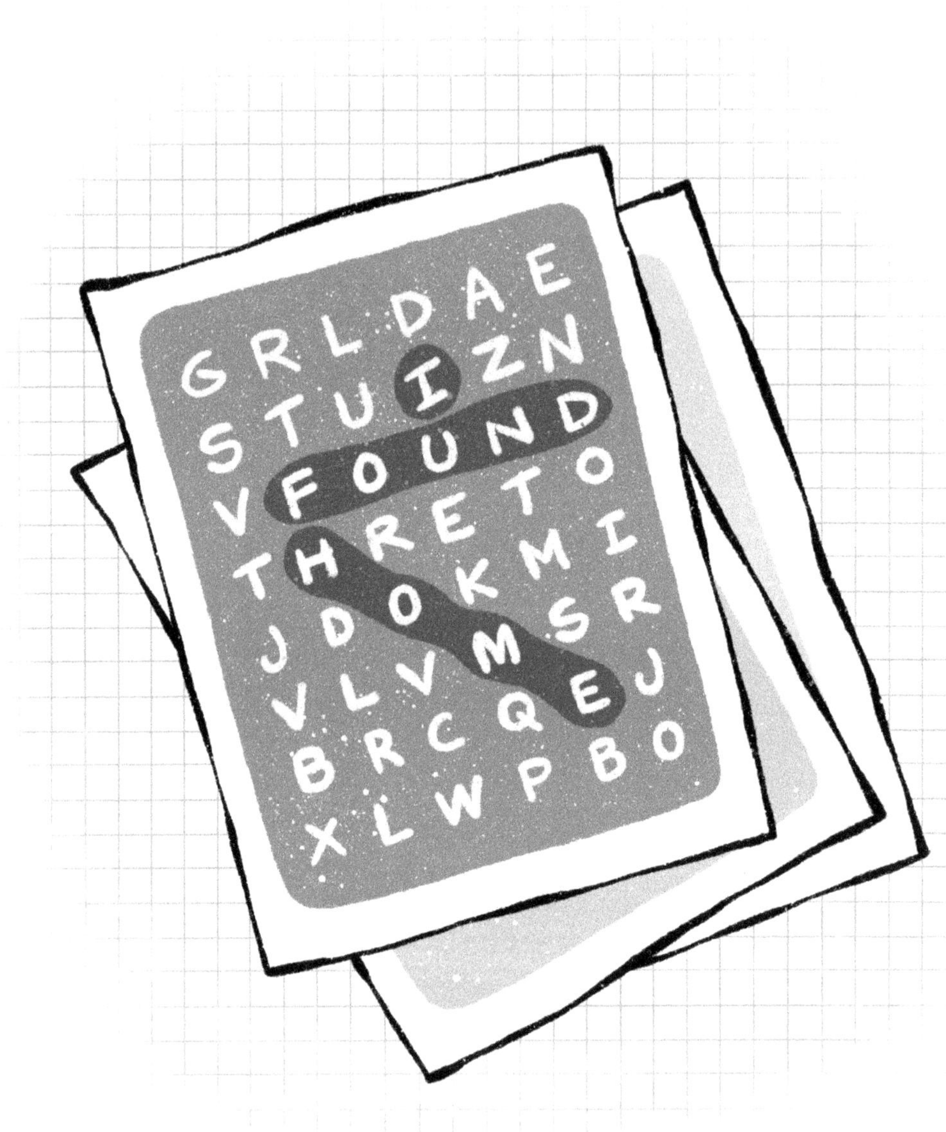

G R L D A E
S T U I Z N
V F O U N D
T H R E T O
J D O K M I
V L V M S R
B R C Q E J
X L W P B O

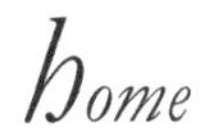

home

and finally, finally,
she found her way home
only to realize
she had never even been gone
home was right here
right where she had been all along

she was home.

Aridam s. dojie

Aridam is a writer, poet, and artist hopelessly in love with *love*. She has been making art ever since she could hold a crayon between her pudgy toddler fingers, and has forever been obsessed with stories and words that rhyme.

When not writing, reading or drawing, she's usually lost in daydreams or found annoying her cat at the speed of a hundred-kisses-a-minute.

*M*ore from the author

Visit https://www.asdojie.com to know all about Ari's upcoming releases, ARC opportunities, merch, freebies, and more. Or find her on social media (instagram, threads, twitter/x, youtube, and pinterest) as @asdojie